A Life of Ethics and Performance

A LIFE OF ETHICS & PERFORMANCE

Edited by Dr. John Matthews & Dr. David Torevell

A Life of Ethics and Performance
edited by John Matthews and David Torevell
This book first published 2011
Paperback edition with colour plates 2013

Cambridge Scholars Publishing

12 Back Chapman Street, Newcastle upon Tyne, NE6 2XX, UK

British Library Cataloguing in Publication Data
A catalogue record for this book is available from the British Library

ISBN (10): 1-4438-4178-1, ISBN (13): 978-1-4438-4178-8

INTRODUCTION

John Matthews & David Torevell

In the narrative of one very famous ethical life, Christmas day is the *first day*. In the "ripping yarn" of another famed tale of life and ethics, it is almost the last: Christmas Day 1820, Henderson Island, South Pacific Ocean. A group of mariners who have hauled themselves and their battered boats over the rocky shores of this remote and uninhabited island fretfully hunt for food. Exhausted, dehydrated, starving and having found little to eat and no sustainable or reliable source of fresh water, the sailors reluctantly acknowledge that, having only recently found land they may have to take to their battered and barely navigable boats once more.

Five days earlier the malnourished crew of the whale ship *Essex* sailing out of Nantucket spied land at Henderson after drifting at sea for over a month. In under a week the exultation of the crew at spotting land had subsided to despondency as they realized that Henderson could not sustain human life. Stove by a whale on November 20th 1820 in the incident that would inspire Herman Melville's *Moby Dick,* they had gathered what food and water they could from their broken and sinking vessel before setting off in three whaleboats in search of land and rescue. Having been rammed by the whale almost exactly at the equator and with the Galapagos Islands approximately 2000 miles to their east, the nearest inhabited islands where they might be saved were the Marquesas. With the strong west-flowing current and the mighty southeasterly trade winds their frail whaleboats could reach the Marquesas in a matter of days or perhaps weeks and thus long before their supplies ran out. However, Captain George Pollard, advised by his First Mate Owen Chase and Second Mate Matthew Joy took the fateful decision to sail a course for Chile and the East coast of South America, over 5000 miles away as the crow flies and almost double that distance along the course that the currents and winds would ensure they would take. The *Essex*'s Cabin Boy, Thomas Nickerson, who would, as one of the survivors of the ordeal, go on to write a memoir of the disastrous voyage, later described this decision as a "fatal error" and asked "how many warm hearts have ceased to beat in consequence of it?" (in Philbrick, 2007: 97). During the course of what would turn out to be an over-90-day voyage to South America nine men would die, all would suffer extreme dehydration and starvation, one would go insane and the surviving crew would be reduced to cannibalizing their shipmates. The reason Pollard, Chase and Joy elected to fatefully shun the nearby Marquesas? Their fear that cannibals inhabited the islands.

Without a satisfactory Christmas feast and having witnessed how the man-of-war hawks on Henderson island robbed the tropic birds of their food, and fearing that the same situation might play itself out aboard the whaleboats as meagre resources dwindled further, three of the crew now on Henderson Island, Chappel, Wright and Weeks, decided to remain as their shipmates once again embarked for South America. Their judgement proved to be prophetic and, having consumed the emaciated remains of those who starved during the voyage, on February 6th 1821 the remaining crew of one of the whaleboats took the decision to draw lots. The proverbial short straw fell to a boy called Owen Coffin. After reassuring his shipmates that he "liked it [his lot] as well as any other" (in Philbrick, 2001: 176) and after he had imparted a message to Pollard (his cousin) to give to his mother should he survive to see Nantucket, Owen Coffin laid his head on the gunwale of the boat and was dispatched with a shot from the Captain's pistol. Coffin was soon butchered and consumed and no doubt as his sparse remains failed to satiate his shipmates the remaining men in the boat must have eyed each other uneasily, wondering whose turn it might be next to lay their head on the gunwale.

The fateful story of the crew of the whale ship *Essex* and the profound ethical dilemma they faced on February 6th 1821 inspires Andy Park's illustration that adorns the covers of this book. The familiar peaks and troughs of the sea-waves appear to stretch out forever beyond the edges of the book, much as they must have stretched out interminably for the shipwrecked crew of the *Essex*. The great isolating power of the sea over human creatures of the land is emphasized in the monotonous and limitless rippled lines. The irony that, upon the limitless sea that divides and separates civilizations from one another, the crew of the *Essex* should become what they feared most is perhaps the most poignant detail of their story, especially given that the Captain and his mates were simply misinformed.

Captain David Porter of a US Frigate also called *Essex* had sent reports from his voyage via the Marquesas in 1812 to say that "in times of famine . . . the men [of the Marquesas] butcher their wives, and children, and aged parents" (in Philbrick, 2007: 95) and Captain Georg von Langsdorff who had alighted there eight years previously had observed that the natives found human flesh so delicious that "those who have once eaten it can with difficulty abstain from it" (in Philbrick, 2007: 96). No doubt it was these and similar reports that informed Pollard, Chase and Joy in their decision to avoid the Marquesas. The irony of placing themselves in such dangers to avoid cannibals and, in so doing, to become cannibals is compounded by the fact that modern day anthropologists have cast doubt on Porter and von Langsdorff's accounts. Viewing Andy Park's drawing with this in mind the mournfulness of the oceans comes to the fore; the oft-drawn parallels between seawater and salty tears, crying rivers and oceans. A special association between the sea and mourning is a common theme in theatre: it gives a plot to Synge's *Riders to the Sea* and the poet and radio-dramatist Dylan Thomas utilized this association to great effect in *Under Milkwood* where a chorus of dead seamen return to visit their old captain from the orphan-making and all-widowing sea. In the example of the death of Ophelia, the inscrutable and implacable waters inspire a moral discourse on suicide between Hamlet's mother, Ophelia's brother, a priest and a church sexton (from the Latin *sacristanus* meaning "custodian of sacred objects").

A further irony of the *Essex* tale is that in that great isolating sea where the men of the *Essex* found themselves so terribly alone they were in fact *surrounded*. Their much-missed Nantucket loved ones were not physically present but, in a sense, omnipresent during their voyage and especially during their moments of fraught decision-making. Nathaniel Philbrick's historical account of the *Essex* disaster recalls Pollard's distress when Owen Coffin drew the short straw. Pollard offered to let his head take the place of Coffin's on the gunwale – an offer Coffin refused – and no doubt felt deep distress as a consequence of participating in the execution and consumption of his younger cousin. One dimension of Pollard's distress was no doubt the prospect of having to deliver Coffin's message to his mother, Pollard's aunt, and inform her that the son she had entrusted into her nephew's care was now inside his belly. Thoughts of their loved ones invaded the minds of the *Essex* crew constantly and at no times more so then when taking this decision: "what would they think of me if they could see me now?"

This aspect of the *Essex* story is in Andy Park's illustration too: turn the book in your hand to read the back cover and the image of the sea is inverted. The peaks and troughs of the sea-waves become the headrests of so many auditorium seats all facing at *you*. This image casts its viewer in a leading role and thrusts him or her on stage and disconcertingly though the seats are all empty – just as the Nantucketeers' loved ones were all absent – the presence of a critical audience is powerfully summoned. Like the *Essex* crew who feared the Marquesas and their "inversion of the natural order" (Philbrick, 2007: 96) the inversion in Andy Park's cover design reiterates the ethical question facing Pollard and his crew: "what would they think of me if they could see me now?"

This form of questioning and its summons to an absent, impartial and idealized "spectator" or "observer" has been part of ethical philosophy since at least as early as the eighteenth century and the work of Adam Smith and David Hume. Many of the essays in this work concern themselves with the ethical dimensions of spectating and theatre and performance offers an especially fertile territory in which to unravel these enquiries. Furthermore, the auditorium uncovered in the inversion of the sea-image infers a stage and *actors* on it. This theme too – how one should *act* – is a central question proposed and addressed in the chapters that follow and in this collected exploration of performance and ethics. As I noted at the outset, Christmas day is, in the biblical narrative, the *first day*. The biblical narrative is a story of *Life* and also of *a life*: from creation in the Garden of Eden to destruction in the revelations of St John and from birth in a manger to death on a cross. The biblical narrative has given much impetus to ethical thought and the reference made to it in this work reminds us that ethics is not really about isolated choices – such as that taken by Pollard – but about the context and continuing consequences of each choice taken. Ethics is a question about how to act but it is also, as Adrian Heathfield has observed, concerned with the "timeless . . . question; 'how to live?'" (2001).

This book, *A Life of Ethics and Performance*, is not about how to live "the good life" but rather how standards of "goodness" are negotiated at different times of life and what any such negotiation entails. Its emphasis on the theatrical and performative reminds ethical philosophy that *being good* is in an important sense a matter of *acting good* and that acting good is a question of *performing* (or *not-performing*) certain roles and duties. The chapters of this book are loosely modelled on the "seven ages of man" motif and chart a selection of ethics from conception to birth, to childhood, adolescence, adulthood, middle age, to old age and the experience of dying. The book also extends this motif and recalls the biblical narrative, which has been so central to ethical thinking, by beginning with a meditation on conception and concluding with some thoughts about afterlife.

References

Heathfield, A. 2001. 'Coming Undone', in *It's an Earthquake in my Heart: A Reading Companion.* Chicago, IL. Goat Island.

Philbrick, N. 2007. *In The Heart of the Sea.* New York. Harper Perennial.

1

A PROLOGUE

Nicholas Ridout

The task: to write a prologue to a book comprising essays I have not read. The rule: to make no assumptions about what they contain. The response: to hazard a few guesses as to the circumstances under which such a book on ethics and performance might have been imagined. The hope: that I will neither coincide so absolutely with what is written in the pages that follow as to appear redundant by means of repetition, nor be so wide of the mark as to become redundant by means of irrelevance.

How to act? How to live? The distinction between these two questions might rest upon spectatorship. To act is to decide, to appear. It might be possible, though, to live without acting. To live, as it were, the unexamined life, not, apparently, worth living. The moment one imagines one's life to be examined, even if the examiner is none other than oneself, one's life becomes, in a manner of speaking, a kind of act. It offers itself up for the attention of others; it poses as exemplary. This quantum of self-regard turns over the living of the good life to the apparatus of the theatre, surrenders it to calculations of effect and affect. Thus it is that the life not worth living – the life that performance affirms against the pretensions of its double, the theatre – is the only life of which an ethical claim might be made. This seems to be true whether the ethical claim is articulated in either Kantian or Levinasian terms. For Kant, the surrender to calculation would be the disqualification, because for Kant, to act ethically is to act entirely disinterestedly, without any regard whatsoever for the attention of others and what they might think or judge. For Levinas, the very articulation of the claim might be unethical, in its non-recognition of the subject's infinite responsibility to the Other, as exemplified in the attention, in this account of the good life, that it pays to itself. One would be very tempted to abandon both Kant and Levinas, from the beginning, then, were it not for the greater temptation of considering the question of the life not worth living in relation to both ethics and performance. Before the beginning, then, it's back to Socrates.

> Some one will say: Yes, Socrates, but cannot you hold your tongue, and then you may go into a foreign city, and no one will interfere with you? Now I have great difficulty in making you understand my answer to this. For if I tell you that to do as you say would be a disobedience to the God, and therefore that I cannot hold my tongue, you will not believe that I am serious; and if I say again that daily to discourse about virtue, and of those other things about which you hear me examining myself and others, is the greatest good of man, and that the unexamined life is not worth living, you are still less likely to believe me. Yet I say what is true, although a thing of which it is hard for me to persuade you. (Plato)

What might Plato intend by having Socrates speak of a life not worth living towards the end of a rhetorical performance which seems to be a matter of life and death? Only seems, though, as the trial is a foregone conclusion. A rhetorical performance, then, that seems, but is not, a matter of life and death. Socrates, we know from the beginning, will be condemned to death, since the only way for him to avoid this fate would entail his renouncing the philosophical (examined, theatrical) life. It would be, in other words, to accept a life not worth living. To return to the question of Plato's intention (as if that were a proper question), perhaps it is to help us understand that in this situation – a trial – a life is precisely what is under examination, and that the life in question and at stake – Socrates's – is a rhetorical performance, even if it begins, as is customary on such occasions (courtroom dramas, weddings, retirement parties), with a disavowal of performance capacity. The trial, then, the occasion for this performance, is also the condition under which life becomes worth living. And life itself takes the form of an *Apology* (for a life worth living). The life worth living is the life for which one can perform an *Apology* by means of living the life. Presumably this life is the exemplary life. Which suggests that it might not be entirely facetious to consider the heroic and exemplary figure of Socrates, embracing death in the name of the life worth living, as an early exponent of durational or endurance performance: a kind of Tehching Hsieh of the fifth century BC. This seems more interesting, at least, than to think of the performance artist as a latter-day tragic hero.

Both of these parallels might seem to participate in a kind of classicist exclusivism, in which ethics *tout court* is imagined as having been handed down from the antiquity of a single culture, as though the Greeks (whoever they were) had started everything. This tendency is perhaps especially acute in the field of theatre and performance studies, in which this kind of origin myth still holds surprising sway. The tendency tends to a lockdown once we start thinking about the relationship between theatre (or performance) and ethics, just as it does when we are trying to do the same thing with our politics. The myth of a simultaneous birth – of theatre, of politics as we understand it, and, pushing it, perhaps, but all the same, ethics too – not only radically limits our capacity to think the complexity of our cultural inheritance (as Settis [2006] argues so persuasively), it also invests too heavily in coincidence. An egregious example of this first error – the error of cultural limitation – is to be found in Ridout (2009), in which an exclusively Western or European conception of *both* theatre and ethics *and* the link between them seems to lie not too deep below the surface. Ridout would have done well to consider some of the postcolonial critiques of this tendency mobilized by Page duBois (2010).

DuBois (2010: 5) cites Dipesh Chakrabarty (2000) coolly noting that "I am aware that an entity called 'the European intellectual tradition' stretching back to the ancient Greeks is a fabrication of relatively recent European history". She goes on to identify the extent to which "even the most enlightened of classicists" – she refers here to Jean-Paul Vernant to whose work both duBois and Ridout clearly owe considerable debts – exhibits this tendency, albeit with some mitigation. DuBois writes of Vernant's characterization of "Greek civilization", that it demonstrates "the great virtue of dethroning the Greeks from their pedestal as the point of origin of human civilization *tout court*, but also the limitations of a Western perspective that sees the Greeks as autonomous and isolated from the Near East, Africa, and India, a perspective now eroded by our situation within globalization" (DuBois, 2010: 15). While duBois' project is to open up the field of classical studies to an understanding of the historical reality of the ethnic, religious, linguistic, sexual and cultural diversity of the "civilization" of which it speaks, Settis seeks to expand our sense of what "the classical" might mean, so that it encompasses both "classical" moments in cultural histories other than Europe's and also the structures of return in which the idea of "the classical" is produced in the writing of history: "We have to look to the 'classical' not as our dead and unmerited inheritance, but as something profoundly remarkable and *alien* that needs to be recreated everyday and something that is a powerful incentive to understand 'otherness'" (2010: 111)

My first guess, then (and about time, too), as to why we might be interested in exploring the relations between ethics and performance today, is this: Perhaps it is a way of simultaneously satisfying our desire for cultural continuity, while at the same time troubling that desire itself by naming it as exclusionary myth. The recognition of the myth as exclusionary is itself an ethical recognition, if ethics might be understood as bearing some substantive relation to the conceptions of "hybridity" (duBois) and "otherness" (Settis). That is to say, in a context where there is a pervasive understanding of ethics as grounded in one's relations with others, it is our ethical reservations about our own cultural mythology that make the ethics-performance coincidence so appealing. The idea of undermining the association between ethics and performance appeals directly to our sense of what it might mean to act ethically.

To associate Socrates with Tehching Hsieh might then be a case of repetition with a difference. It might start out as the rhetorical subordination of a Taiwanese artist to the power of the exemplary "European" philosopher. It might reappear as a provocative anachronism in which the life of the Athenian is read as a kind of artistic practice, in which the Athenian's absention from writing and his appearance as merely a character in the writing of another makes him look like a rather surprising fountainhead for a culture which would like to imagine its world domination to have sprung from the nib of a pen rather than the point of a sword or the barrel of a gun (but not, perhaps, from one which might make performance its privileged mode of communication). It might also strike a third time, asking whether the association of the Taiwanese artist and the Athenian ascribes to the artist a genealogy which is not his own, and thus, in the process, reads his work under western eyes only, obscuring genealogies which might be more, well, Taiwanese. In this third strike a fourth already sounds: to insist upon not making this association is to promote the essentialist myth once again, this time in the form of the idea that one can only make sense of oneself in relation to a single cultural inheritance, defined in terms of nation or ethnicity. Why think of Tehching Hsieh as Taiwanese at all? Or Socrates as Greek, for that matter? Whatever happened to elective affinities?

Perhaps another reason (and let this be the second guess) for the current interest in the intersection between ethics and performance might have something to do with the direction taken by ethical thought in the latter part of the twentieth century. Or, to be more precise: the theoretical humanities of the late twentieth and early twenty-first centuries have welcomed a new kind of ethical thought whose language, if nothing else, seems to offer terms in which performance and performance scholarship might speak of itself. This is attributable partly to the influence of Levinas, of course, whose language of responsibility towards the Other, conceptualized in the encounter with the "Face", has been enthusiastically taken up in recent scholarship in performance studies (in most cases, somewhat after its appearance in literary criticism, for we students of performance are almost always after the event). But a more general sense of the possibilities of an ethics that attends to relations between subjects rather than the relations of subjects to norms also seems to appeal. Thus acts of spectatorship start to be fraught with new kinds of ethical considerations: in place of what might perhaps be described as a moralizing or ideological critique of spectatorship – a censorious blend of Debord and Prynne (of *Histrio-Mastix* not *Her Weasels Wild Returning* fame) – there has emerged a discourse of witnessing, responsibility, intimacy and care in which both makers and spectators (among them writers and scholars) have learned to speak of what they do. This is not just a matter of Levinas, as relayed by Derrida, nor even of the influence of Derrida's own ethics, but rather a consequence of two far more pervasive assumptions which shape everyday thinking about ethics: the sanctity of human life and the freedom of the individual. And above all, the routine assumption that these two principles amount to one and the same thing.

There is also some degree of complementarity to be found in the ways both this kind of ethical thought and performance might conceive of themselves as experimental practice: operating not in accordance with the law, but in the mode of hypothesis, in the experience of the event and in a spirit of openness to the future, to that which will come. This is ethics for the liquid subject, the subject in constant becoming. It is an ethics deeply invested in human potentiality. This means it is never far from struggle between the interests of the individual and those of whatever group (community, multitude, class) the individual might become in relation with. So this is not just a matter of language; it is also a question of politics. And the question of politics might be posed as follows: What has happened to politics in all this ethics? A third guess, then, as to what might be at stake here, could involve wondering to what extent the ethics adopted by performance studies might or might not be a form of politics, and suggesting that an interest in thinking things ethically responds to certain contemporary difficulties with the political.

This third guess, then, might be made as a speculation that follows directly from the historical proposition of the second: what I referred to earlier as "the direction taken by ethical thought in the latter part of the twentieth century". In this respect it is hard not to make a fairly explicit connection between the specific contribution of Levinas's philosophy and the general conditions of receptivity to this contribution, on the one hand, and the disaster of the Nazi genocide on the other. Levinas's philosophical project might be understood as an attempt to begin the work of philosophy all over again. If the historical catastrophe of the Nazi genocide is understood as a consequence of the way in which modern Europeans had come to think about the world – as one in which human life could be disposed of altogether in the interests of a supervening but deranged "rationality" – then the undoing of such a way of thinking becomes an urgent ethical task, for philosophers and their publics alike. In starting all over again, Levinas places both the temptation to murder and its prohibition at the centre of the encounter with the Other, and makes the coming into being of the Subject, by way of the encounter with the Other, a matter of assuming full responsibility for the life of the Other. The injunction not to kill, when to kill might be possible, even desirable, is, in this sense, the foundation of subjectivity. The face of the Other is "exposed, menaced, as if inviting us to an act of violence. At the same time the face is what forbids us to kill . . . The face is what one cannot kill, or at least it is that whose meaning consists in saying: 'Thou shalt not kill'" (Levinas, 1985: 86).

This constitutes a central element of what Howard Caygill (2002: 2) refers to as Levinas' "fragile response to political horror" – whose fragility is far from being a feebleness or inadequacy –which clearly has its origins in a specific political situation, and, as a response to that situation, may readily be understood as political. However, some adaptations and developments of this ethical relation, including several within the field of performance studies, either imply or openly press a critique of political action. In its more radical forms such adaptations of Levinas would argue for the value of certain modes of passivity in relation to political situations, or, if not passivity, an active abstention from action – usually on the part of privileged Western/Northern actors – on the basis that an active intervention would constitute an act of authoritarian violence. Given the longstanding investment in "efficacy" on the part of many scholars and practitioners within performance studies, this presents something of a dilemma. A powerful impulse to do something (and after all, performance is the field of action), to bring about change, to make things better, to transform, finds itself counterposed by a similarly powerful impulse to abstain from action. Does your responsibility to the Other make you an activist or a witness? In many situations this is by no means a simple choice, and the range of possible decisions and their ramifications is what constitutes the ethical and political landscape for numerous ethnographers, NGO workers, and, yes, government agencies too.

For this is not simply an issue for those of us interested in performance. Indeed, it may well be the case that articulations and experiences of this ethical situation arising from the practice and study of performance derive from our immersion in a more general contemporary political paradigm, which a commonsense view of ethics as concern for the rights and well-being of others predominates. This is perhaps best encapsulated in the problem of "humanitarian intervention", where the paradigmatic concept of "human rights" is deployed, both sincerely and cynically, to motivate or justify various forms of intervention in defiance of international conventions on sovereignty. The familiar leftist critique of this state of affairs is exemplified by Slavoj Žižek (2005: 128):

> So, to put it in the Leninist way: what the "human rights of Third World suffering victims" effectively means today, in the predominant discourse, is the right of Western powers themselves to intervene politically, economically, culturally and militarily in the Third World countries of their choice, in the name of defending human rights.

Less familiar than this kind of denunciation, however, is the way Žižek develops this, dialectically, to suggest that the commonsense ethics of concern for the other which underpins and legitimates such political intervention thus performs precisely the kind of violence against the subjectivity of the other that the foundation of such an ethics sought to make its central prohibition:

> The moment human rights are thus depoliticized, the discourse dealing with them has to change: the pre-political opposition of Good and Evil must be mobilized anew. Today's "new reign of ethics" . . . thus relies on a violent gesture of depoliticization, depriving the victimized other of any political subjectivization. (Žižek, 2005: 128)

Or, to put it bluntly: an ethics whose origins lie in the command "Thou shalt not kill" has found a way of justifying murder. Which is an old story.

It is tempting to consider the "depoliticization" that appears to constitute this "new reign of ethics" in relation to the crisis of the communist project. Whether "communism" in its twentieth-century form came to an end with the fall of the pro-Soviet regimes in Europe in 1989, as is generally assumed, or in 1968, when the legitimacy of the communist parties and orthodox Marxism in Europe was challenged by radical alternative forces on the left, the absence of a single ideological project with universal ambitions (with the exception, it should be noted, of feminism) clearly made space for the emergence of a differentiated range of political movements, nearly all of which actively sought to distance themselves from the supposed 'violence' of a single transformative ideological project. In doing so many such movements adopted and developed ways of thinking and speaking about politics in which questions of difference emerged as central, alongside very careful calibration of subject positions and a renewed emphasis on personal authenticity. While Žižek may view, and rightly so, the mainstream appropriation of an ethics of alterity in the service of the economic interests of 'Western powers' as an attempt to do away with politics altogether in the name of ethics, it would be unfair to extend this critique to the continuum of post-1968 radical movements, for whom the emphasis on difference and plurality rather than universalism contributed to new ways of thinking and doing politics, rather than a retreat.

What is lost, and often deliberately repudiated, in this way of doing politics, is the idea that collective action can best be undertaken by means of a community that defines itself in terms of its self-identity. What is to be gained, then? The question of how one might think and proceed on this basis lies at the heart of Jean-Luc Nancy's *The Inoperative Community*, in which he affirms that

> there is . . . no form of communist opposition – or let us say rather "communitarian" opposition, in order to emphasise that the word should not be restricted in this context to strictly *political* references – that has not been or is not still profoundly subjugated to the goal of a *human* community, that is, to the goal of achieving a community of beings producing in essence their own essence as their work, and furthermore producing precisely this essence *as community*. An absolute immanence of man to man – a humanism – and of community to community – a communism – obstinately subtends, whatever be their merits or strengths, all forms of oppositional communism, all leftist and ultraleftist models, and all models based on the workers' council. (Nancy, 1991: 2–3)

For Nancy, then, political action both grounded in this kind of community – in the form, say, of the political party – and seeking the realization of a society modelled on such an idea of community, might be understood as deficient in terms of both efficacy and ethics. Efficacy, because such an idea of community is inadequate to the reality of human relationality and thus provides a faulty vehicle for action. Ethics, because the coercion involved in the formation of such a community, as either strategy or *telos*, constrains the potentiality of relations between and among us (and not, it has to be said, between "individuals", because, for Nancy, the individual is itself a product of the very "community" he wishes to avoid). So, crucially, this is not simply the familiar argument that "community" is coercive and homogenizing, and that it restricts the "freedom of the individual" or some such ideological construction. It is, rather, an opening out, beyond both "individual" and "community", towards a mode of relationality in which, somewhat ecstatically at times,

> The presence of the other does not constitute a boundary that would limit the unleashing of "my" passions: on the contrary, only exposition to the other unleashes my passions. (Nancy, 1991: 32–3)

This, it seems to me, does not place the same limits upon action as have recently been developed within performance studies from a reading of Levinas. Instead it seeks to find affirmative value in the passionate exploration of relationality, where others appear as invitations rather than prohibitions. The practice of performance, then, might understand itself and its ethics in terms of its passionate movements, movements that might make you beside yourself, with something or someone.

References

Caygill, Howard. 2002. *Levinas and the Political.* London and New York. Routledge.
Chakrabarti, Dipesh. 2000. *Provincializing Europe: Postcolonial Thought and Historical Difference.* Princeton, NJ. Princeton University Press.
DuBois, Page. 2010. *Out of Athens: The New Ancient Greeks.* Cambridge, MA and London. Harvard University Press.
Levinas, Emmanuel. 1985. *Ethics and Infinity: Conversations with Philippe Nemo.* Pittsburgh, PA. Duquesne University Press.
Nancy, Jean-Luc. 1991. *The Inoperative Community.* Translated by Peter Connor. Minneapolis and London. University of Minnesota Press.
Plato. *Apology.* Translated by Benjamin Jowett. E-Book at Project Gutenberg, http: //www.gutenberg.org/files/1656/1656-h/1656-h.htm
Ridout, Nicholas. 2009. *Theatre & Ethics.* Basingstoke. Palgrave Macmillan.
Settis, Salvatore. 2006. *The Future of the Classical.* Cambridge. Polity Press.
Žižek, Slavoj. 2005. 'Against Human Rights', *New Left Review* 34, July–August: 115–131.

2

PERFORMING LIFE, LIVING PERFORMANCE

David Torevell

This chapter demonstrates how the meaning and significance of the paschal mystery in Christianity, and its relatedness, according to St John (10.10), to living life "abundantly", is best understood within a *performative* rather than propositional framework. It will also outline how offering the salvific mystery of Christ's death and resurrection to the world is experienced most poignantly within the Church's liturgy, for it is in this arena that participants are invited into a dramatic ritual of *anamnesis*, at which they learn to inhabit in their own lives (and bodies) the life and death of the One to whom they pay homage. Above all else, then, Christian worship is concerned with participants' absorption into an event, a happening which is repeated and made present again and again for all time; the consequence is that the ontological changes involved enable worshippers, through their involvement in liturgical performance, to experience a 'fuller' life not possible by their own efforts alone. As Eagleton comments, "religious faith is not in the first place a matter of subscribing to the proposition that a Supreme Being exists, which is where almost all atheism and agnosticism goes awry . . . it is for the most part performative rather than propositional" (2009: 111; Loughlin, 1996; Davies, 2002). This is not to say that any act of faith is independent of the propositional, but it is to suggest, along with Badiou, that genuine ontology only becomes possible by response to an *act,* and that faith is substantially loyalty to an event, an original happening, which disrupts the grain of the world, even if that occurrence is never easily defined or named. Liturgies remind and implicate participants in an event, therefore, and are acted out for all time until the *eschaton*, so that their eventfulness might be internalized and become the bedrock of a different form of life by those committed and obedient to its claims.[1]

Encountering the Event

Let us stay with the French atheist contemporary philosopher Alain Badiou a little longer. He maintains that an authentic life is one lived in loyalty to an event which becomes a revelation to be esteemed and followed, since it turns the tide of history by its originality and counter-cultural insistence. A passionate allegiance to any such event is necessary for a new type of living and being to emerge, since ethical living is determined and maintained by such loyal commitment. Badiou is concerned, therefore, to outline an ontology which stems from a notion of an "event" which calls for a strong response of commitment which has the aura of a "fidelity", rather than a passing or casual following. Events which generate such allegiance are "truth events" and are most likely to emerge from the sites of love, art, science and politics. The kind of fidelity such truth events invite and demand is not tame, but disruptive and startling; it "is not a matter of knowledge. It is not the work of an expert: it is the work of a militant" (2007: 329). By this he means ethical living entails the radical following and exploration of the effects of a significant happening, involving the performance of a "militant" life in connection to such an event. "Militant", he avows, "designates equally the feverish exploration of the effects of a new theorem . . . the activity of St. Paul, and that of the militants of an *Organisation Politique*" (ibid.). St Paul's activity comes about because he is part of the "militant" response to the event of Christ's life, death and resurrection, the paschal mystery. This brings about a new way of seeing and acting in the world, or what Badiou sees as another mode of discernment. Consequently, the constitution of the subject is connected to an individual's intense loyalty to a world-changing event, who perpetuates it through her witness of staggering allegiance. It is described thus: "The operator of the faithful connection designates *another mode of discernment* : one which, outside knowledge but within the effect of an interventional nomination, explore connections to the supernumerary of the event" (ibid.). Such loyalty demands a distinct type of activity and beckons one to "perform the minimal gesture of fidelity . . . The actual meaning of this gesture – naturally depends on the name of the event . . . on the operator of faithful connection" (ibid.: 329–330).

Although Badiou's theory situates itself within mathematical discourse, a strong performative element can be discerned in his writings. His work on ethics, for example, borrows from Lacan's idea that "all access to the real is in the order of an encounter" (quoted in Burns, 2009: 29) and in *Being and Event* he writes that any minimal gesture of fidelity as referred to above, "is tied to the *encounter* between a multiple of the situation and a vector of the operator of fidelity" (Badiou, 2007: 330). Badiou's atheistic position becomes evident in his belief about the relationship of the event to its source; there is no "One" from which matter emerges, only the void. What there is instead, is an endless series of multiples, which all emerge from nothingness. The only foundation that exists is void or absolute nothingness. Nevertheless, his view of fidelity signals a notion of "infinity" when the effect of and loyalty to, an event is generated over time and when eventually culture assimilates it into its folds and it becomes normalized. He writes "the generic procedure of fidelity progresses to infinity" and "entails a reworking of the situation; one that, while conserving all of the old situation's multiples, presents other multiples" (2007: 342). This in turn "*forces the situation to accommodate it*: to extend itself to the point at which this truth . . . attains belonging, thereby becoming a presentation" (2007: 342). Consequently, "anonymous excrescence in the beginning, the truth will end up being normalized" (2007: 342). As such, art, love, science and politics really do change the world when others act in fidelity to them: "the all-powerfulness of a truth is merely that of changing what is, such that this unnameable being may be, which is the very being of what-is" (2007: 343). The subject is then brought into a new order of truth borne by the commitment to the ideals of an event. Faith, in this Badiou sense, articulates a loving commitment to an event.

It will be helpful at this stage to consider how we might read the event of the paschal mystery in the light of Badiou's claims. We begin with some differences. Significantly, liturgy's re-enactment of an event entails participation and solidarity with the event in the present, at this moment in time, now, not the mere commitment to a set of ideals which stem from an event of the past; *anamnesis* entails participation in an event in the present as worshippers are drawn mystically into the body of Christ's ongoing redemptive action (Ratzinger, 2000). It is also important to realize that when St Paul refers to the Christ-event, he means an event which continues to make its mark on his identity over time. Barclay makes the point that when St Paul writes "I have been crucified with Christ. It is no longer I who live, but Christ who lives in me" (Galatians 2.19–20), he is using the Greek perfect tense which communicates what has been and *continues to be*: "The Christ-event is not only a singular interruption in the once-and-only past; it keeps puncturing the folds of time to re-enact the new creation" (Barclay, 2010: 177). Furthermore, Badiou's claim about the "non-place of place, the void" (2007: 111) is replaced by the liturgy's insistence on the event of the death and resurrection of Christ, the life-giving event which comes into being now, in the present. If there is darkness then there is always allegiance to the light which emerges out of its presence; the void of Good Friday is the entry into plenitude. It is also the case, as O'Neil Burns astutely points out, that the "revolutionary" subjectivity liturgy forms is far more radical than Badiou's, for it involves a willingness to perform acts of martyrdom, of laying down one's own life as well as living in allegiance to an event: "Rather than political subjects willing to kill, the liturgy forms subjects willing to die. These subjects willing to give their lives out of fidelity, known as martyrs, are subsequently those who are most faithful to the event inaugurating their subjectivity" (Burns, 2009: 33). The cost, therefore, of following the event liturgy performs is far higher than Badiou's, I think. A further difference is the somatic incorporation of liturgical participants into the redemptive body-event of Christ and his Church; it is to this major difference that I now wish to turn.

Performance of Liturgy as *Disciplina*

Let us take an example of this distinctive embodied approach to religious performance from the *Rule of St Benedict,* which became the most authoritative model for monasteries in the Middle Ages and beyond. The Rule employed the Latin word *disciplina,* which is a translation of the Greek word *paideia* which in the Old Testament referred to divine education directed towards a whole people and which in liturgical and patristic texts reflected the process and methodology of teaching as well as the content of what was taught. It also referred to divine knowledge, physical and spiritual practice, an organized community, the authority of the Abbot and measures necessary for the attainment of Christian virtues (Asad, 1993: 137). But for our purposes it is vital to see how discipline was inextricably linked to the practice and performance of the divine office and to the disciplining of the body. For example, Hugh of St Victor's instructions to his novices demonstrate the unbreakable interweaving of bodily discipline with the formation of Christian virtue.

> It is discipline imposed on the body which forms virtue. Body and spirit are but one: disordered movements of the former betray outwardly *(foris)* the disarranged interior (*intus*) of the soul. But inversely, "discipline" can act on the soul through the body – in ways of dressing (*in habitu*), in posture and movement (*in gestu*), in speech (*in locutione*), and in table manners (*in mensa*) . . . *Gestu* describes outwardly a *figure* presented to the gaze of others . . . even as the soul inside is under the gaze of God. (Quoted in Asad, 1993: 138; Burton-Christie, 1993)

This is an important point for it signifies that the disciplinary regulation of the body through ritual practice is indispensable for bringing about Christian virtue. For new novices into the monastery it was essential that they began to learn, through daily practice, the importance of ritual expression and deportment, both within liturgical contexts and outside them. For example, the dignity, decorum and poise of the body, inside and outside the sanctuary, was an important practice for teaching virtue and for ongoing spiritual formation.[2] Once the body started to learn how to bend and genuflect, to bow and kneel, how to serve at table and treat guests as if they were Christ himself, then attitudinal change could begin to take place. Such formative change involved understanding, feeling, desire and will and the disciplinary ritual procedures, conformed to as if to the authority of a law, in this case the Rule of St Benedict, determined what had to be done, by whom and at what time, in order for this transformational change to take place.

The Rule, therefore, was essentially a text of discipline, and a reflection of God's divine law and it brought about within novices the beginnings of an internal change rooted in humility underpinned by an ascetic and stringent lifestyle rooted in the body.

What is also noteworthy is that the written texts chosen by the monasteries became an aspect of the disciplinary practices themselves and were never separated out from bodily practices. Texts were part and parcel of the everyday ritualized routine – the scriptures and writings of the Early Fathers were read during meal times and in chapel, *lectio divina* pondered upon in individual monastic cells. They were literally part of the performance of daily monastic living. Sacred words were chanted, recited, read, proclaimed, meditated on by the monks and performed not for an audience but for their own virtuous development (Asad, 1993: 141; Jasper, 2009). The Medieval historian R. W. Southern points to how the drama of the liturgy rooted in Scripture spilled over into every aspect of daily monastic living:

> As in the ceremonies of Palm Sunday every incident of the day was a drama, but much more than a drama: in a drama the actor assumes only for a moment the *persona* that he temporarily embodies; but, in the monastic day, these symbolic activities brought an intense experience of the supreme world-embracing reality in which the monastic community lived. Every item in the daily routine of the monastery was a declaration of the presence of God and of the whole company of heaven: it was theology in action. (Quoted in Martin, 2008: 99)

The scriptures which were read, sung, listened to and pondered upon meant that distinct biblical images became absorbed by the body and the senses with the result that participants became formed by their narratives and symbolism.

This inculcation of the virtues through a disciplined performance of the text and body was taken outside monasteries and became part of the ongoing liturgical practice of the wider Church as the Body of Christ became built upon the performance of scripture interwoven with the bodily enactment of the sacramental rites. Reading and listening to the Word became a bodily and performative exercise and the annual cycle of the biblical readings was to become a ritualized performance of the Word, as scripture became the enduring text written on the heart of all Christians (Torevell, 2009: 25–29).

Performing the Text

Just as the monks were formed through ritual practices which included the public reading of scripture, so, too now, Christian communities become attuned to the cadences and rhythms of the faith though their bodily attentiveness to the Word performed repetitiously over liturgical seasons and time. Earlier forms of digesting scripture consisted of reading whole books from the beginning to the end; worshippers simply picked up the narrative from the earlier reading. Now *lectio selecta* is the norm, but the aim is the same: to allow the words to inform the heart and to be changed by the embodied performance of scripture, its regulated repetition over a three year cycle, which begins to attune those listening to the values to which the scriptures refer and by being engaged in its performance, allowing one to live according to the distinct ethical cadences and rhythms of the Christian faith. As Fodor (2004: 161) puts it, "What begins to occur in these subtle and complex movements is that slowly, steadily, indelibly the reading community becomes marked by, attuned to, and conversant with the distinctive rhythms, accents and cadences of the faith".

Here one might say that one is being (in)formed into a distinctive ethos of the Christian tradition through a performances of the Word. Such performances of the Word are maintained by dramatic devices as the text is situated within carefully chosen spatial positionings, gestural features, processional alignments and all in relation to the architectural settings which set it apart and enable it to communicate its unique and dramatic role in the formation of the Christian conscience. Just as the bread is broken, shared and digested, so too is the Word. Performance is never primarily cognitive, but entails a gradual assimilation of the text into our bodies, as we eat the words offered as a gift to us and chew over the words of scripture that they might inhabit our deepest being and transform the heart (Torevell, 2009). Liturgy, therefore, is always a form of training, entailing for worshippers a gradual assimilation and "incorporation" into the enfleshed liturgical Word; worshippers then become embodiments of the Word in the communities they serve, particularly those which are dispossessed and marginalized. Being part of a public absorption of the scriptures brings about an inculcation, training, and exercise in scriptural reasoning which better enables a life of faithfulness which is identity-constituting and character-building. There is a fundamental and existential reorientation involved here, as participants become incorporated into the communal life of faith, freely allowing themselves to be attuned to the harmony of the Bible – to the deep structure of language with its "virtually endless modulations" (Fodor, 2011: 161). Liturgy always entails this kind of re-learning to live and to be and enables participants to become a new body in and with others who share their embodied ideals.

Liturgical Living – A Creative Non-place

I want now to move on and examine briefly how the notion of the daily performance of liturgical living as proposed by the contemporary philosopher-liturgist Jean-Yves Lacoste in his *Experience and the Absolute* (2004). In delineating an answer to the question what it means to exist liturgically, Lacoste calls our attention to the differently-oriented experience of life after baptism. He suggests it entails living in a "non-place" since such existing seeks no hold over the Absolute nor manipulates it into existence; it is a world between the provisional and the definitive. But the "non-place" is not the kind of void envisaged by Badiou.

> The liturgical non-place is well deserving of its name. Refusing to be solely defined by his historicity, and symbolically subverting his relation to world and earth, he who prays is symbolically nowhere. He is refused the parousiacal proximity of the Absolute; he refuses to participate in the dialectics which make up history; and he declares the phenomenological ground of his historality powerless to determine what he ultimately is. Thus does he live the tension between the provisional and the definitive in his worldly encounter with the Absolute. (1994: 54)

Lacoste asks:

> How, then, are we to exist within the horizon of an absolute future that is not our death and that we can anticipate only by admitting the most radical of disparities? Liturgy wishes for the *eschaton.* It proves this by endeavouring to disqualify every temporization governed by being-in-the-world and (thus) by our being-towards-death: by endeavouring to subordinate care to restlessness and facticity to vocation. (2004: 85).

The *eschaton* is not brought about in what Lacoste calls the non-place and non-time of liturgies, but it does have an impact on our world and makes the present "tremble" (*en inquiétant notre présent*); thus "the Absolute enables us to effectively infringe on the laws governing worldly temporalization" (2004: 85). The person who prays "acts as the negation and the adoption of a position: it denies that the logic of inherence unveils all that we are, and it affirms our desire to exist before God" (2004: 44). The world now ceases to envelop us and we begin to acknowledge that the world holds no more promise for us, as we lose interest in its presence in favour of another presence (2004: 44). We start to exist before Him who is to come (2004: 44); living liturgically is living with the "expectation or desire for Parousia in the certitude of the nonparousiacal presence of God" (2004: 45).

Such a person "leaves many things behind him, starting with the profanity of the world . . . he also takes leave of every relation with the real in which appropriation is an essential moment" (2004: 174). The world always keeps God and his nonparousiacal presence veiled over (*dans l'inévidence*) (2004: 46). This is the tension of liturgy and allows us an experience turned towards God while waiting for the definitive unveiling of the Absolute (2004: 46). Although this waiting might be characterized by restlessness and indeed boredom, there are moments of peace which appear as if one were experiencing the parousia itself. As Lacoste writes:

> Liturgical vigil . . . the chiaroscuro of the world is dissipated and where man can at intervals enjoy (*jouir de*) the presence of the Absolute as if he were enjoying his Parousia. Restlessness does not prevent definitive peace from reigning over our present in advance (*par anticipation*). (2004: 85)

Liturgical living is partly understood by Lacoste in relation to the kind of place the person who prays allows himself to inhabit. He is symbolically absent from the world and wishes to take definitive leave of the dialectics which make up history. This experience of liturgical being Lacoste calls "violent", since it comes about as humanity wrenches and places itself outside its own self-induced existential framework and begins to see that the limits of existence are not the limits of humanity: "Only a certain violence enables man to exist before God. Man liturgically exceeds what he is initially; the limits of the existential are not the limits of his humanity" (Lacoste, 2004: 105). But as well as the experience of a different location, there is also the experience of a different time : Besides being a "non-place", liturgy is also a "non-time", a time to nullify the self's preoccupation with itself. It demands an attentiveness (*d'une attente et d'une attention*) but the vigil is time gained (Lacoste, 2004: 83). This experience is one of dispossession for the liturgical subject: "Nothing they could have in their possession contributes to the expression of their identity, and they are offered nothing they can take possession of" (Lacoste, 2004: 174).

For Lacoste, liturgy encourages us to generate a moral concern for the world for it offers a distance from the vantage point of the *parousia.* He writes: "it must be recognized that liturgy and the diversion in which it engages open up a determinable path to the exigencies that the 'daily' play of being-in-the-world obliterates" (ibid.: 73). The liturgical arena allows us to imagine our being in the world as another type of liturgy where our moral consciousness can be played out. Any such moral concern "derives its incisiveness from the universal reconciliation for which liturgy is the symbolic and inchoate space" (ibid.:74). After we return to the earth after liturgical experience liturgy holds its sway: "Because of the eschatological surplus provided by liturgy, the dialectic of world and earth sees itself enriched by a third term, that of the Kingdom" (ibid.: 74). Although liturgy is a non-place which provides one sort of homeland, it is also in the world that the eschatological homeland – the Kingdom – "is implicated inchoately (and thus in a non-symbolic way) in the world as soon as men see themselves as brothers" (ibid.: 74). Liturgy does exacerbate our not being at home in the world but this should not be a cause for concern. For this unease reveals to us that it is only possible to respond satisfactorily to our place in eschatological terms. Such feelings of unease "preside over the opening of the worldly non-place in which the eschatological contents of signification proper to the humanity of man are unveiled" (ibid.: 74). Lacoste summarizes his position: "We must finally, dare to say that liturgy enables us to dwell in the world and on the earth by superimposing on our facticity the order of an ethical vocation that alone authorizes us to let the Kingdom invest itself in world and earth in advance" (ibid.: 74–75).

A New Performance

This performative dying to the old self and expectation of the parousia is clearly emphasized in the rite of baptism. Rather than stressing the eradication of original sin, the rite in its earliest forms demonstrates how the birth of a child needs another birth – this time "in Christ". The performance of baptismal liturgy was the drama of the beginnings of a new life, a performance which would be repeated through the receiving of the sacraments throughout life, especially the Eucharist. The child becomes consumed by the first performance of the biblical text as it learns its first steps in living it out; the future is an ongoing discipline of "doing" and performing the baptismal text in everyday life, enabled and strengthened by the nourishment of the sacraments themselves. This is a formation into an ethical vision of life where self-giving means self-fulfilling.

This first baptismal rite is thus the beginning of a series of performative acts including and emphasizing the body. Baptism is an incorporation into

Christ's body which entails entering mystically into His death and resurrection; it brings about an incorporation into His body which is the Church and mystically unites the child with Christ's life and death so closely that one learns to leave the old unbaptized body behind as one enters into a new corporeal existence. The body in turn learns to re-situate itself to a larger body, the Church, of which Christ is the Head. Baptism is never, therefore, a private act, but is always a public proclamation of the beginnings of a Christian life rooted in the Word of the text and made real in the body through the sacramental life of the Church, a series of events which are re-enacted from birth to death.

According to St Paul, it is the Holy Spirit which builds up the body of Christ through baptism (1 Corinthians 12.13). But this first performance is simply the beginning of the ethical life and a life given over to the Spirit. The Catholic Church, for example, believes that at baptism, the first signs of the theological virtues – prudence, justice, fortitude and temperance – are given though the power of the Holy Spirit and God's grace (Roman Catholic Church, 1994: 1267). The incorporation into the Church means that participants start to learn how to subdue the differentiated and alienated self and learn to give themselves over to one People, where all barriers of race, class and gender are broken down. As the Catechism states, "From the baptismal font is born the one People of God of the New Covenant, which transcends all natural or human limits of nations, cultures, races and sexes: For by one Spirit we were all baptized into one body" (ibid.).

Here begins the *performance of a life* given over to a reconstituted ontology since the baptized no longer lives for herself but for and in Christ who died and rose for her. The baptized, therefore, have a new ancestry, as sons and daughters of God – and in this, their identity and ongoing sacramental life resides. But this is no ordinary handing over, but rather a dramatic transference due to the archaic nature of liturgy itself, which entails releasing strong reservoirs of remembrance and harnessing power to overturn unjust human structures (Kavanagh, 1990: 40–42); as I mentioned earlier, worship teaches the body to belong to a community dedicated to *anamnesis*, the assembly's remembering and re-enactment of events which "jerked the world definitely onto new courses" (Kavanagh, 1990: 4). It is a body in constant dramatic encounter with the forces of darkness, dissolution and death. The only witness is the cold slab of the altar of sacrifice; false liberalism comes easily and is never apposite (Eagleton, 2009: 24). Therefore, "The coming of the kingdom involves not a change of government, but a turbulent passage through death, nothingness, madness, loss, and futility" (ibid.). There is no possibility of a smooth evolution here. Given the twisted state of the world, self-fulfillment can ultimately come only though dispossession and those living this new life are renewed throughout their lives that faith in the powerless which can come to power is not in vain (ibid.: 27). The body they must unite with is a disfigured body: "The traumatic truth of human history is a mutilated body, a body which has associated itself with *anawim* – the scum of the earth. Jesus dies in an act of solidarity with the *anawim* – the scum of the earth" (ibid.: 23). The living of the performance then is a voyage into madness, absurdity and self-dispossession. The God of the Old Testament reminds those who perform its words that Yahweh Himself "is homeless, faceless, stateless, and imageless" and One "who prods his people out of their comfortable settlement into the trackless terrors of the desert and who brusquely informs them that their burnt offerings stink in their nostrils" (ibid.: 56)

This tortured death therefore, is part of the life-giving performance of baptism. The corpse's shroud is also the baptismal garment and both garments dramatize the same paschal event. There is no interruption between birth, life and death since baptism, the sacramental stages of life and the liturgy of the dead allow an incorporation into the body of the risen Christ which was once dead. As life unfolds, the Eucharistic narrative is performed and eaten; what more bodily identification with the paschal mystery is possible than this? As the Catechism declares, "The Eucharist – story and meal, praise and performance – is the gift of Christ, and Christ, – the Body of Christ which is Christ-and-the-people-of-Christ-incorporated, inscribed in Christ's own story – is the gift of the Eucharist" (Roman Catholic Church, 1994: 226).

Conclusion

Consequently, the Christian life is always the ongoing performance of the paschal mystery; it is the living of a performance entangled somatically and inextricably with the performance of Christ's life, trying always to remember and instantiate the text which was performed at birth and which gives the capacity to live life "abundantly" for all time. The faithful performance of such a Christian life enables the one who has died to "depart this life marked with the sign of faith, with his baptismal faith, in expectation of the blessed vision of God – the consummation of faith – and in the hope of resurrection" (Roman Catholic Church, 1994: 1274). Here reside the fruits of sacral life-long performance.

Notes

1 The relationship between liturgical practice and memory rooted in strong ritual structures is a theme I have addressed at length in Torevell, 2000 (especially 190–193). Here I suggest that the performance of the body is particularly suited to securing stable remembering since it plays a central role in ritual enactment and harnesses prescribed somatic behaviour. Such practices are appropriate to mnemonic activity since they rely on a bedrock of scripturally based performativity, whereby the events of salvation, repeated again and again until the end of time, sustain the collective memory (Connerton, 1995). As I comment in relation to the Roman Catholic tradition, 'For centuries Roman Catholic liturgy kept this tradition of introducing its ritual participants to a permanent and universal metanarrative to be told until the end of time. Through its ritual retelling of the story of Christ, it developed the means of offering each member of the Church a part in the performance of its own sacred drama. . . . By participation in the rites of the Church, the congregation became no longer witnesses of the drama but characters within it, learning to adopt the character of Christ. This was no mere pageant, but an experience of *anamnesis*" (Torevell, 2000: 191–192).

2 The same emphasis on the body was also prevalent in the educational outlook of the cathedral schools of the Middle Ages. There was a distinct correlation between the control of inner impulses and control of the regulated body. As Jaeger indicates, "The motion of the body is perhaps the most visible means of registering the inner state: the way of gesturing and walking (external *motus*) indicates the way of feeling or the inner state (*motus animi, status animi*)" (Jaeger, 1994: 10). Outward signs of inner virtue were demonstrated through clothes, gestures and their bodily deportment and poise.

References

Asad, T. 1993. *Genealogies of Religion: Discipline and Reasons of Power in Christianity and Islam.* Baltimore. John Hopkins University Press.

Badiou, A. 2007. *Being and Event.* London. Continuum.

Barclay, J. 2010. 'Paul and the Philosophers: Alain Badiou and the Event', *New Blackfriars* 19(1032): 171–184.

Burns, M. O'N. 2009. 'Alain Badiou and the Event of Liturgy', *Anaphora,* 3(1): 25–34.

Burton-Christie, D. 1993. *The Word in the Desert: Scripture and the Quest for Holiness in Early Christian Monasticism.* Oxford. Oxford University Press.

Connerton, P. 1995. *How Societies Remember.* Cambridge. Cambridge University Press.

Davies, D. 2002. *Anthropology and Theology.* Oxford. Berg.

Eagleton, T. 2009. *Reason, Faith and Revolution: Reflections on the God Debate.* New Haven. Yale University Press.

Fodor, J. 2011, 'Reading the Scriptures: Rehearsing Identity, Practicing Character' in Hauerwas, S. and Wells, S. (eds). *The Blackwell Companion to Christian*

Ethics. Oxford. Blackwell: 155–169.
Jaeger, S. 1994. *The Envy of Angels: Cathedral Schools and Social Ideals in Medieval Europe, 950–1200.* Philadelphia. University of Pennsylvania Press.
Jasper, D. 2009. *The Sacred Body: Asceticism in Religion, Literature, Art, and Culture.* Waco. Baylor University Press.
Kavanagh, A. 1990. *Elements of Rite.* Collegeville. Liturgical Press.
Lacoste, J.-Y. 2004. *Experience and the Absolute: Disputed Questions on the Humanity of Man.* New York. Fordham University Press.
Loughlin, G. 1996. *Telling God's story: Bible, Church and Narrative Theology.* Cambridge. Cambridge University Press.
Martin, D. B. 2008. *Pedagogy of the Bible: An Analysis and Proposal.* Louisville. Westminster John Knox Press.
Ratzinger, J. 2000.*The Spirit of the Liturgy.* San Francisco. Ignatius Press.
Roman Catholic Church. 1994. *Catechism of the Catholic Church.* London. Geoffrey Chapman.
Torevell, D. 2000. *Losing the Sacred: Ritual, Modernity and Liturgical Reform.* Edinburgh. T&T Clark.
Torevell, D. 2009. ' The Sacred Space of the Heart and the Modern University', in Brie, S., et al. (eds). 2009. *Sacred Space: Interdisciplinary Perspectives within Contemporary Contexts.* Newcastle. Cambridge Scholars: 23–38.

3

BEING YOURSELF

Adam Hosein

Introduction

More or less everyone has been told at some point in their lives that they ought "to be themselves". Sometimes it's said to provide relief: "Don't worry, just be yourself". Other times it's more critical: "Who are you trying to be?" Whatever the tone, these speakers are trying to convey something normative; that it's somehow *better* to be yourself. In this chapter I'm going to ask what exactly is meant by this advice and then will consider whether it is *good* advice, whether there is any virtue in being yourself.

Let's start by looking at a few examples, taken from "high" and "low" art, of people considering questions about who they are and what it takes to be authentic. First, though, let me say a few quick words about my methodology. In what follows I hope to use these examples to illustrate some features of commonsense and philosophical ideas about authenticity. It is common in philosophy to use "thought experiments" to evaluate theories, and examples from art can provide us with especially subtle examples for this purpose. Given this end, it will be well to read the characters in the relevant texts as if they were real people.

Here are the examples:

Hamlet

Ophelia's father, Polonius, believes that Hamlet is becoming crazed and thus dangerous. Polonius asks her to cooperate with him secretly to discover the source of Hamlet's apparent affliction. Probably realizing that she is following her father's orders, Hamlet berates Ophelia for various failings, feeling betrayed by her. But he takes Ophelia's corruption to be a symptom of a widespread disease and soon turns his criticisms on women in general. Among his central complaints is that women refuse to be themselves or to act authentically: "I have heard of your paintings too, well enough; God has given you one face, and you make yourselves another" (Shakespeare, 2006: III.1.150). Polonius himself emphasizes the importance of authenticity elsewhere in the play: "to thine own self be true" (Shakespeare, 2006: I.1.78).

John Tucker Must Die

Three friends feel wronged by beloved high-school sports star John Tucker because he has promised each of them romantic commitment.

They collectively attempt to exact revenge on Tucker by enlisting another girl, Kate, who has previously been peripheral to high-school social life, to break Tucker's heart. Kate begins to succeed in wooing Tucker and, in doing so, becomes a part of the clique of popular girls. But she is soon warned of the dangers both of her mendacity and of her change in personality: "Be careful who you pretend to be, you might forget who you are."

A Streetcar Named Desire

Blanche has been chased out of the town where she was born and had worked as a schoolteacher because of a series of scandals. She is now "visiting" her sister Stella and her husband Stanley. Blanche acts as if she were still in work in her home town and avoids mention of the scandals. She carries herself in the manner of an upper-class Southern woman wedded to contemporary norms of feminine grace. Stanley challenges her on this identity and her past.

Mean Girls

Cady, who has been home schooled in Africa for her life thus far, enters a high school for the first time and is thrust into a more typical American adolescent social life. She tries to fit in with this new crowd and, in doing so, adopts some of their petty jealousies, meanness and so on. Her parents confront her about this change: "Who are you?" The movie ends with an affirmation of the virtue of being yourself as Cady learns to return to some of the values she learned before high-school.

Authenticity: The Basics

It will probably not have escaped your attention that all the subjects of criticism in all of these examples are women and I think this is somewhat representative. As appears in the Hamlet quotation, women are often singled out as supposedly being especially likely to be inauthentic or to live for others, be they men, members of their high-school clique or society at large. And, as the familiarity of the high-school movie tropes illustrates, the advice or complaint that you should be yourself is also especially likely to be told to teenagers in our society, who are often considered especially in danger of "losing themselves".

So, we are extremely familiar with "be yourself" as a piece of advice or a complaint. But what exactly does it mean? Schematically, I think the form of the command goes something like this.

First, there is some set of norms *N* that the person being commanded is currently acting in accordance with (at least to some extent). We can think of the norms as themselves a set of commands of the form "You should do *X* under circumstances *C*." So, for instance, the girls in the high school movies might be acting in accordance with a set of norms associated with membership in a certain clique and these norms might include commands such as "You should wear certain kinds of clothes when you are attending school," "You should attend parties thrown by boys in the sports teams," etc.

Secondly, there is another different set of norms *M* which the speaker thinks the listener ought to comply with instead. So, for instance, the teen girls in the movies are advised to adopt the behaviour of a studious individual, following rules such as "You ought to do your homework," "You ought to attend mathematics club" and so on. Or the norms might be those of an "ordinary" American girl, who listens to her parents, is less concerned with being popular and so on.

Thirdly, it is claimed that you ought to comply with the second set of norms because doing so is more authentic, more *you*. The girl who follows the clique is performing, pretending to be someone she isn't, whereas the girl who listens to her parents and does her work is being herself.

So much for the basic structure of claims about authenticity. The difficult, and puzzling, question is what *makes* the preferred set of norms *M* the ones that are a better fit with authentic behaviour or the ones compliance with which would express the true self. Why is staying home to study the real girl in action, whereas going out partying is the fake? Which is the face that God gave Ophelia and which is the mask she has put on? In what follows I'd like to survey some possibilities about how to draw this distinction.

Authenticity as Naturalness

One intuitive idea about the authentic and the inauthentic is that to find the former one need only try to avoid complying with norms that are *social* expectations and instead look to follow just the *natural* norms that apply to you. There are some norms people follow because a certain culture or society has produced the expectation of acting in accordance with them. There is a contingency to these norms and expectations: each society and culture produces its own, different version. But there is another set of natural norms that we can divine by abstracting from the various social norms that happen to surround us.[1]

This distinction between the natural and the social seems to me entirely bogus, for reasons that will be familiar to those who work in performance studies. When we are thinking about how to act, the place we start from is by considering how others around us behave. We look at common models of behaviour in our society and consider which we would like to follow. Of course, there is also room for innovation: one can dislike certain patterns of behaviour and try to modify them. But our starting point is always with the modes of life that surround us. We should be very wary, then, of a view which says that there is some alternative way of deciding what to do which draws not on existing social norms but on some other "natural" ways of behaving. There is no reason at all to suppose that we have access to any such non-social source.[2]

Thus, when someone tries to convince us that a certain set of norms should be followed because it is more natural, all they can really be expressing is their own preference that we follow those norms rather than others. And this seems to me dangerous because while such a person is simply trying to convince us to follow their preferred set of norms they typically do not see the need to defend them. Calling some norms the natural ones is a way of avoiding the need to give any defence of those norms or to give reasons for thinking they are superior.

Consider Hamlet's attack on Ophelia. Ophelia is torn between various competing demands that she is trying to reconcile. She wants to obey her father and do what she thinks is best for the state but she also wants to respect Hamlet and the love they have shared. Hamlet accuses her of corruption, of behaving in accordance with social norms but not authentically. But he offers no reasons why she should behave in the way he wants her to and does not engage in any consideration of her dilemma. Calling her actions unnatural is a way of criticizing her without having to offer any such defence. It is, in effect, mere bullying. In private moments, Hamlet is forced to question his certainty ("The spirit I have seen / May be a devil") and we too have to question his authority to make these judgements.

It's a familiar claim in political theory that appeals to authenticity can pave the way to totalitarianism.[3] A government that claims to know what is a subject's authentic interest, as opposed to just what the subject herself thinks is best, authorizes itself to coerce citizens to act in certain ways even where the individuals themselves are entirely against those acts. We have seen that claims about authenticity can play a similar role in more personal interactions, making it possible for one individual to browbeat another without engaging with her own views.

Authenticity as Self-Control

There are other kinds of appeal to authenticity that avoid this sort of domination. The problem with appeals to the natural, we saw, is that they involve an attempt to supplant the judgement of the listener with the judgement of the speaker, to get the listener to act in a certain way without engaging her reason. But sometimes we try to convince someone to act in a certain way precisely by engaging with what they themselves care about. We try to argue with them that being true to themselves requires certain behaviour because this is the behaviour they themselves most value. We might call this "authenticity as self-control". So, for instance, in the teen movies we looked at it is common for the parent or concerned friend to point out to the protagonist that they themselves care about being academically successful, honest and so on but are acting in ways that conflict with these values. The complaint is that the individual is acting in accordance with some norms *N* even though she herself is committed to a different set of norms *M*. Consider a person who is dealing with an addiction. We can imagine them stealing money from someone to buy, say, alcohol and afterwards reflecting that "I wasn't myself when I did that".[4] Although they are acting like someone who thinks stealing is acceptable they do not really endorse this claim.

How does this kind of conflict arise? If someone really cares about being academically successful, for example, won't they act in ways that reflect that value? A long tradition in philosophy is devoted to this question of how it is possible to think it would be best to act in a certain way whilst in fact acting in some other incompatible way and many different answers to it have been proposed.[5] One answer, for instance, is that while we may believe that a certain way of acting is best, our desires may still lead us to act in a different manner. So while we may think it is good to be honest our desire to be popular might lead us to dishonesty. Another possibility is that we fail to do what we think is best when we cannot follow through on our intentions, when we are "weak willed". This isn't the place to review, let alone judge, the long discussion of these issues. For present purposes, what matters is that to fail to be yourself, in the sense at issue, is to fail to live up to an ideal that you yourself endorse. This means that when we criticize someone for being inauthentic in this sense we do not ignore their own views, as we might when appealing to the "natural". In fact, we criticize them precisely by pointing to some aspect of their own view that they are failing to act in accordance with.

Furthermore, authenticity as self-control seems to be an attractive ideal. Those who are unable to control themselves will be unable to reliably do the right thing since even if they come to believe the correct set of ideals they won't have the discipline to follow through. It also seems unattractive in itself to be unable to live up to one's own ideals. We often say that such people have "betrayed themselves", expressing the lack of respect we feel for anyone willing to give up on what they themselves think is important. The person who deliberately does not follow her own ideals is also criticized. This person is often thought deceptive because her actions may give the impression that she endorses norms different from the ones that she in fact accepts.

Self-reliance

So, we have found a way of criticizing people for being inauthentic, for not being themselves, that seems more acceptable and an ideal of authenticity that appears to be valuable and attractive. I have called this "authenticity as self-control". It is this kind of authenticity that is celebrated at the end of the teen movie, where the protagonist eventually finds the strength to act in the ways that she thinks best. Yet there is something about these triumphant endings that strikes us as hollow and sentimental. Why is this? There is something, we have seen, to the ideal that these endings celebrate, so what is wrong with their celebration?

Such teen films typically present a view that all that is needed for authenticity as self-control or as autonomy is a resolute character. They focus solely on the individual's internal struggle to define herself in a way that meshes with her own conception of what is best. The obstacles to her success are largely within her own psychology as she battles with her own desires and so on to achieve authenticity. On this picture, achieving authenticity requires great *effort* but, crucially, it is more or less without *cost*. The teen who returns to the way of life her parents and friends endorse and which she, at least at one time, endorsed, must make a serious effort of will to return to her old way of life. But once she does so she is better off in nearly all respects: she is more popular, more successful, more happy and so on.

It is this aspect of the teen movie that is in great tension with the teen life of any actual person.[6] For we know that actual people are moved to act not just by their own ideals and will to act on them but by the many pressures placed on them, whether consciously or not, by others and thus the costs of acting one way rather than another. The actual teen, as is sometimes briefly acknowledged even in the teen movie, is subject to serious social sanctions if she adopts some behaviours over others. Acting in the ways that she values by, say, working hard or disobeying conventions of social life in the school, might result in serious threats of disapprobation and even violence.[7]

Williams' Blanche de Bois is a more extreme example. She is repeatedly berated by Stanley for acting in accordance with norms that she cannot genuinely think are important. For instance, he points out that she makes a pretence of acting like someone who believes that women must be chaste even though, he claims, her past behaviour suggests she does not really believe in ideals of chastity. Throughout the play Stanley pressures her to be authentic by not acting in accordance with ideals she does not endorse, to "Lay . . . her cards on the table" (Williams, 2009: 21).

Stanley's reprimands ignore entirely the reasons why Blanche acts as if she cared about chastity and so on. She acts in this way to avoid serious *costs*, both social and psychological. As an older woman with no job, income or emotional support, Blanche finds herself in need of a husband who might help provide her with these things. But she will only be acceptable to a prospective husband if she can convince him that she does believe in ideals of feminine chastity and so on. Otherwise, she will be considered "not clean enough" (2009: 89). These are costs associated with how other people will view Blanche. But acting as if she were a person who believed in ideals of chastity and so on is also essential to Blanche's own fragile psychology. Even though she may not fundamentally believe in such ideals any more, Blanche still wishes to consider herself the sort of woman who does. It is thus not only destructive to Blanche when other people begin to recognize her true beliefs but also when she is forced by Stanley to confront them herself: "And take a look at yourself! . . . What queen do you think you are!" (2009: 94). In the end, Blanche pays the enormous price of psychological breakdown.

It thus seems to me that there is a dark side even to authenticity as self-control. Appeals to authenticity of this kind do not license the kind of domination involved in appeals to the natural. But they can still be destructive when we ignore the costs people must endure to follow the values they endorse. Not all failures to follow those values are mere failures of will; many are responses to serious costs and pressures.

Notes

1 I am indebted to Appiah's (2004) discussion for this way of drawing the distinction.
2 Appiah makes a similar point.
3 See "Two Concepts of Liberty" in Berlin (1969).
4 I borrow this example from Frankfurt (1971).
5 The classic source of this problem is Aristotle (2002).
6 I don't mean to suggest that the teen movie, or "low art", in general fails to represent the world well, or less well than "high art". I just find the particular tension I've discussed striking and a helpful guide to some of our blind spots in thinking about authenticity.
7 Mill (1869) also stressed the significance of social pressures on our actions.

References

Aristotle. 2002. *Nicomachean Ethics.* Translated by R. Crisp. Cambridge. Cambridge University Press.

Appiah, Anthony. 2004. *Ethics of Identity.* Princeton, NJ. Princeton University Press.

Berlin, Isaiah. 1969. *Four Essays on Liberty.* Oxford. Oxford University Press.

Frankfurt, Harry. 1971. 'Freedom of the Will and the Concept of a Person', *Journal of Philosophy* 68(1): 5–20.

Mill, John Stuart. 1869. *On Liberty.* London. Longman, Roberts and Green.

Shakespeare, William. 2006. *Hamlet.* Edited by Ann Thompson and Neil Taylor. London. Arden Shakespeare.

Williams, Tennessee. 2009. *A Streetcar Named Desire.* London. Penguin.

4

BEING TOUCHED

Anna Furse

> Touch is not a private act. It is a fundamental medium for the expression, experience and contestation of social values and hierarchies. The culture of touch involves all of culture. (Classen, 2005)

We live in a time of powerfully conflicted feelings about human touch. Touch is complicated. It operates on many physiological dimensions and involves also affect, emotion and consciousness, hence that ambiguous word "feeling" and what it brings to human experience. The entanglement of the somatic with the imaginative saturates touch with cultural meanings that include sexuality, conviviality, custom, health, vulnerability, violence, and taboo. Touching between humans is always a communication experience and, when not violent, abusive or unwarranted, expresses empathy, a reaching out *to be in contact*: I want to suggest how in training the body, working with touch's complexities, we might reconcile "sense" with "sense", how a *Weltanschauung* can be embodied by practitioners of moving-in-contact – certain martial and dance artists – and I want to suggest some ethics involved. In foregrounding examples of what I would cite, from my own experience (and predilection) as "good practice", I hope to indicate how ethical values are *inscribed in*, rather then *described by* the moving body.

Ethics are principles of virtue and morality that affirm what we consider to be good, and within a contemporary frame this would comprehend values such as fairness and egalitarianism that might be conducive to conviviality. Stanislavski devoted an entire chapter to what he calls a creative "atmosphere" he understood as "ethics, discipline, and also the sense of joint enterprise" that is "*not the creative state itself*. . . but [which] prepares and facilitates that state" (Stanislavski, 1988: 249). Alan Read, a century on, takes Michel de Certeau's assertion that ethics "defines a distance between what is and what ought to be. This distance designates a space where we have something to do" and applies it to theatre. "Both ethics and theatre", suggests Read, "are concerned with possibility" (Read, 1995: 90).[1] He isn't talking about all theatre. He isn't talking about dramatic literatures or representation ("the reflection of an existing proposition"). He is talking about performances that make sense of everyday life, that work with "possibility without closure". I understand this space where the ethical process can be unfurled, or made to occur, as one in which the body itself, inside and out, is the "something to do", something potential but not yet defined, that is of itself both "creative state" and "atmospheric" (in the sense of tone, mood and attitude) and certainly full of possibility:

> imagery is fleeting. *What remains is the continuing sense of the body's potential to invent and discover*, to recover equilibrium after losing control . . . Paxton's dancing . . . reminds us that the body's grace is rooted in its extraordinary varied repertoire of capabilities. (Banes & Alexander, 1980: 70, emphasis added)

Bodies aren't static in either form or content. While classical culture codifies physiques and physical expression into fixed propositions of grace and beauty, living beings are in a perpetual condition of biological change. As if to archive this life cycle, bodies store memory. Karl Marx's aphorism "the forming of the five senses is a labour of the entire history of the world down to the present" (Classen, 2005: 61) posits that the body carries its history somatically and accumulatively and exists therefore in a state of potential transformation. He suggests thereby ways in which "aesthetic forms both produce sense experience and result from it" (Howes, 2006: 59); in short, culture *is* the expression of human history, art reflecting and altering both our *sense* of the place we occupy in the world around us and what this is made of. A constantly evolving dialogue is at work between our bodies, external reality and how we interpret both and as Merleau-Ponty[2] holds, the body is "our means of communicating with [the world]" (2004: 106): we receive information *via* its thresholds: surfaces, orifices, senses, only to process the affects from and within it, translating these into expression again. This occurs at all speeds, both unconsciously and consciously all the time. And this is what artists do, whether with pen, brush, keyboard, clay or other humans *to hand*. We are outside-in/inside-out, a mobius strip of information-processing, our senses honed, each of which possesses a particular, and interrelated, topography. Skin is the topography of touch, both organ and medium; it is the first point of touch.

In the haptic arts we use the tactile sense as a text.[3] Touch turns us outwards towards others, reveals us to them, as well as the reverse being also true: it turns us inwards, reveals them to us. Touch tells; it can demystify;[4] it disarms, bypassing ego, and the narcissistic need for admiration (what Grotowski called "publico-tropism" and Stanislavski one of theatre's negative "bacilli"). Touch brings us down to earth, tenderizes the hard skins we develop to protect ourselves emotionally and physically in a competitive world, neutralizes our differences, permits us to *rub along together*. I would argue that such effects might constitute an "ought", indicating a constructive way of cohabiting with others. If our bodies practise conviviality-in-motion in studio, might this not provide a template for living? Certain haptic practices give form to cultural alternatives in specific physical training activities that, in turn, *incorporate ideology*. Working with touch doesn't only require ethical conditions to work in but actually promotes an ethical creative environment that is variously receptive, responsible, respectful, generous, independent, gregarious, communicative, public spirited and *involved.* Touch *ipso facto* involves closeness and by implication this includes the optical close-up. Western culture has, conversely, privileged objectivity and distance since the Renaissance when both the vanishing point in art and anatomical dissection in medicine elevated a *perspective* on nature and the world, not a commingling with it (even if that perspective is itself deceptive and ideological: it was a geometric *trompe l'oeil* (tricking the eye) designed to affirm the prestige of the private owner's position of power over the artefact and his judgement on its composition, that in turn gave it value as a commodity). Hockney's abiding interest in perspective is demonstrated in many works including his remarkable film lecture on an ancient Chinese scroll (Hockney, 1988) that, as he unravels, tricks the observer's point of view in ways that are devoid of Western mathematics of perspective in art.

As Foucault has repeatedly insisted, political control cannot function without optical distance and the body is institutionally subject to taxonomy, regimes and techniques of repression, pain and punishment. "The Gaze" in Foucault's discourses on power holds the powerless in its grip. Panopticism (the apotheosis of duality between controller and controlled) systemically ensures that "all the authorities exercising individual control function according to a double mode; that of binary division and branding . . . and that of coercive assignment . . . [and with] *constant surveillance*" (Foucault, 1991: 199, emphasis added). Since power is maintained by acuity and from the vantage point of *panorama* (and its inverse, from that of – presumably blurry – *proximity*) we also find throughout human history that the upper classes work with their heads, at a remove, whilst the lower class work with their hands, close-up, touching stuff.[5] There are clean hands and dirty hands, high culture and low culture. Metaphors of heaven and earth, rich and poor, aristocratic and popular culture are vividly expressed in the corporeal, as Bakhtin identifies: in contrast to "classic images of the finished, completed man, cleansed, as it were of all the scoriae of birth and development", the non-aristocratic body is "unfinished and open" and "not separated from the world by clearly defined boundaries; it is blended with the world, with animals, with objects" (Bakhtin, 1984: 26–7) – *terre-à-terre*[6] then, close to nature, unfettered and enjoying itself. These types in turn carry social and political significance, the "open" body linking to the public world of carnival and rituals (subversion of authority) whilst the "closed" links to the authority of official culture, today's "individualised consumer society" (Turner,

2001: 66). Such associations resonate with certain contemporary moving bodies I shall come to, which, whilst not Bakhtin's bawdy Rabelaisian grotesques, are similarly organic, accommodated to human earthiness, populist in principle and embodiments of egalitarian values.

What's Touching About Art

As we have seen above, proxemics in the optic/haptic experience count a great deal for both subject and object, and since our distance from any sensory event affects how we both see and feel, touch can subvert experience and shift our perspective from outside to inside, *the closer we get,* affecting what we see and how we see it, whether in focus or blurred, in detail or the whole picture.

In art we may *be moved* emotionally, spiritually, imaginatively. We call this affective event "being touched". In each use of the verb "touching" (sensory or emotional) the same path from sensation to meaning occurs for the recipient, whether stimulated from tactile or other senses. In art the two "feelings" can conflate because we experience emotions as well as sensations physically. Bachelard speaks of the impact of aesthetics as direct transmission,[7] its visceral resonances and reverberations a "phenomenology of the poetic imagination": "images excite us" (Bachelard, 1994: xxiv) and excitation is corporeal. If aesthetics are visceral, then, metaphorically speaking, the way to a person's heart is through the flesh:[8]

> A photograph's *punctum* is that accident which *pricks me* (but also *bruises me*, is *poignant to me*). (Barthes, 1981: 27, emphasis added)[9]

or

> the work of art of the Dadaists became an instrument of ballistics . . . thus acquiring a tactile quality. (Paterson, 2007: 79)

Whilst the impact of art is felt *via* as well as *operating on* the senses of the receiver, it is normally held frustratingly beyond our reach. In the presence of attractive material forms we regress to polymorphous infants, instinctively desiring to explore with our hands but forbidden to by guards in the public art world. Visitors to early museums were invited to verify their perception of exhibits by handling them (Classen, 2005: 275–85). By the nineteenth century reverence and concern for safeguarding exhibits led to what has become a touching taboo,[10] save for the few and always popular "hands-on" experiences designed for children[11] and often related to science and technology.[12] At *The Titanic: Artefact Exhibition* opened at Discovery Times Square Exposition in 2009, the above ideas, affects and impulses intersect: the *poignancy* of authentic objects salvaged from the wreck on display in glass cases is deeply *touching* because each shoe, tram ticket, plate or purse tells a story of human beings who suffered a sudden and tragic death. The curators have added a huge lump of ice to the exhibits. We are invited to touch this. It has no intrinsic value, except to help verify, through the freezing sensation of our hand encountering its surface, how unimaginably (?) cold it was that night, that ice can be alarmingly sinister. And so we are touched, "pricked" and "hit" by the memorabilia whilst touch-sensing a sample of the natural matter that caused such innocuous objects to become tragic signifiers. This overlapping of feeling with feeling, the ambiguities between our senses, common sense and sensibility is a complexity with which artists can engage.

Towards a Touching Artistic Praxis

Bodies write in space, carry meanings, even where intention is non-narrative. Live performance, and dance specifically, communicates *via* the scenography of the body and involves a great deal of occupational touch, intercorporaeity – the language of conscious touching and being touched – being encoded in any social and choreographic process. In the 1970s touch took on groundbreaking significance in a wilful democratization of dance culture. Postmodern Dance, arising in a USA broiling with civil rights protests, the Vietnam war, the emergence of feminism, liberation movements and radical art movements from Pop to Happenings, sought to replace the richly over-sauced artifice of the mainstream with a franker, stripped down, guileless approach to movement:

> It is my overall concern to reveal people as they are engaged in various kinds of activities – alone, with each other, with objects – and to weight the quality of the human body towards that of objects and away from the super-stylization of the dancer. (Rainer, 1968)

For "New Dancers" (the UK term, developed slightly later, for American 'postmodern dance') and performers it is rarely a matter of social and cultural questions as distinct from the senses. When we focus attention on rules-of-the-game, techniques, methodologies, movement patterns and principles – in any given style or methodology, we are versing ourselves in the knowledge that every action is a choice: to move one way or another. Dance theatre cannot be generalized nor is it value-free. Class, ethnicity, attitudes to gender, beauty, sexuality, physical ideals, are just some of the values a dancer embodies in a vast variety of forms ranging from the social to the artistic, high art and low. Each is meaningful. *How* we move and why – and how we experience our bodies moving in space and with others – constitutes in turn corporeal awareness of the meanings and histories of each form. The dancer knows the exigencies of the style or tradition in which she is working, its lineage and standards of excellence, what she is looking for, expressing. She also knows that the body and mind work *as one* and that the body possesses (*is*) intelligence. Our bodies "know" before we do. "It's like riding a bike" we say when referring to the temporarily forgotten stored memory of learnt physical skills. As Steve Paxton puts it, movement practitioners are in touch with "the good sense of the body" (Paxton, 2010). We know in our bones. We are *thinking bodies* (Todd, 1997).[13]

If we trust in our senses, our bodies' "good sense" and our intuition, precisely how then might the conscious use of touch as a practice and an artistic research include and enfold ethical values? If we comprehend ethical values as connoting just, respectful and socially beneficial principles, what can movement practices possibly tell us about such rational ideas? If haptics relate to sense and sensation, how might we speak of how the haptic and the cultural converge for the practitioner of certain movement arts and how might the spaces in which they are practised and the spaces they describe inform this? I reach for metaphors.

Deleuze and Guattari identify space as "smooth" and/or "striated" (2008: 523–51). Using evocative analogies of text/texture/textile and space in discussing cultural values and forms, in fabrics the striated would be that which is woven, that is, composed of vertical and horizontal elements (warp and weft), is closed on one side (its width) even if its length can be unlimited and has a top and bottom, whilst the fabric of the smooth is *felt* (sic), that is, "an anti-fabric" is "supple", "an entanglement": "it is in principle infinite, open, and unlimited in every direction; it has neither top nor bottom nor center; it does not assign fixed and mobile elements but rather distributes a continuous variation" (Deleuze & Guattari, 2008: 525).[14] In terms of human civilization, the nomad occupies smooth space (in being mobile) rather than the sedentary space of the city dweller (though the city dweller can live nomadically by choice).[15] Deleuze and Guattari's project, whilst emphasizing that the smooth and the striated overlap in nature and in human society ("there are many interlacings"), asserts that smooth space involves "*haptic* rather than optical perception. Whereas in the striated forms organise matter, in the smooth materials signal forces and serve as symptoms for them. It is an intensive rather than extensive space, one of distances, not of measures and properties" (2008: 528). Using this concept to grapple with human movement, the vocabularies I shall be discussing belong semantically to the province of the smooth more than, but not to the exclusion of, the striated.

At the extreme end of dance-art, classical ballet celebrates the mathematics of perspective, the proscenium stage being its architectural manifestation. Its choreography (patterns, lines, repetitions, beginnings, endings, virtuosity) is synonymous with woven fabric, designed for the spectator's pleasure, who receives performances at a proxemic distance that permits overview of the whole stage picture. If a hierarchy is represented on stage by the sequencing and orchestration of a spectacle (from corps de ballet, up to coryphée to soloist to principals, finally to Prima Ballerina Assoluta or Danseur Noble – its aristocrats) this is reflected in the class-system of the tiered Italianate theatre buildings. Cultural meanings regarding class, gender, ability and ethnicity are the warp and weft of balletic narratives and its highly stylized and codified movement vocabulary. This includes all kinds of touch, including the meticulous technique of male-female partnering (based in arduous counter-tensions, balances and lifts) as well as gestures of expressive touch. Ballet compresses and represses sexuality and its values. Expressed in a geometry of rapture, pliability and impossible levitation, the ballet dancer is Bakhtin's classical body *par excellence,* "cleansed . . . of all scoriae of birth and development". He lifts; she flies, light as a feather, on pointe and off, striving to give us the vicarious thrill of weightlessness and ethereality. Her lightness of being makes him seem heavier and *vice versa*. She is perceived to defy gravity, her limbs stretched and folded in a seemingly impossible origami. In the ballerina "the chaos of body transmutes into rational form . . . her movements turn mess into symbol" declares Susan Leigh Foster (1996: 14). Actually, she may not be "mess" and "chaos" at bodily source but, rather, complicated and intricate; but she certainly transmutes, converting organic complication into something leaner, non-reproductive (the ballerina's ideal body is anorexic) and more linear than the layperson can ever be. *In effect, if you get close up* she proves a glittering, untouchable conundrum. She is all projection, as "turned out" in her joints as in her focus on the spectator's gaze, her corpo*reality* camouflaged by the sheer scale of the opera house theatre and its illusion-peddling properties. She is actually sweating buckets, near vomiting with breathlessness and bleeding in her shoes for ballet demands formidable athletic strength disguised as effortlessness. It is, as Margot Fonteyn once remarked, as cruel as bullfights (Money, 1965).

On the other side of the spectrum, in urban life, the ordinary moving-being is also socialized by the striated, with its fixed points, edges, forms, norms. Our bodies are inscribed with the meanings of society's values, as men and as women. This can limit, oppress, straitjacket us. However, as Deleuze and Guattari recognize, we have the choice to be nomadic, even in such a sedentary space; we might choose to live differently, re-evaluate ourselves, transform the spaces we occupy together and our behaviour within these; might we do this *via the body*? For example, if we listen to physical information transmitted at a point of contact between ourselves and another in a safe and non-sexualized environment, we can shift, or at least modulate power relations (e.g. gender) that might prevail in our social lives, and we can do this haptically. A very large, rigidly strong man in an Aikido *dojo* (site of practice) will discover that the dominant role he occupies out in the world renders him surprisingly vulnerable "on the mat". Here, his muscular armour might actually work against him. In Aikido, as in t'ai chi ch'uan (see below), the search is for a deeper, intrinsic energy and power than mere brute force. Like bamboo that nature has designed to survive storms by bending to the winds (in contrast to the thicker, rigid, oak that can be snapped in a blast), he will have to learn to yield – even working with a woman half his size – how to accommodate his own body mass to hers, how to balance forces and use each other for effective movement: *how to move with her.* Conversely, by learning to move in "non feminine" ways, a woman might unlearn all that she has stored in her body as a growing girl. Women have traditionally written with our bodies (Classen, 2005) and are written on (Cixous & Clement, 1986). If "the girl learns actively to hamper her movements" (Young, 1990: 146, 154) in learning her gender role, a New Dancer treats her body as an instrument for research and experience. She will learn to take up space, free her movement, explore organically, dance like a man.

The body contains a mass of information and not all of this is physiological. Much of what we are as embodied beings is acculturated memory and we need to undo this if we seek an authentic way of conducting ourselves in a creative space. Otherwise we risk remaining typecast in hierarchies of power, ego, strength, gender and other roles, repetitions, patterns. In order to adapt – to survive, we learn to awaken our reflexes, be mercurial, adaptable, open, responsive. We might improvise, allow ourselves to touch and be touched, invent possibilities without closure in that aforementioned space where ethics take shape.

Throwing One's Body Into The Fight[16]

Dancers are highly disciplined and generally motivated towards being team-spirited. We speak of the *corps de ballet* ("body of ballet") as the lowest rank in the classical company. We also speak of "esprit de corps" ("spirit of the body") as the feeling of shared loyalty and pride as in times of crisis or military operation for example. This spirit helps at the bottom of the hierarchy whether breaking stones, soldiering or twirling as one of thirty-two swans. It becomes a matter of survival and of keeping your sense of social belonging upwards and out. We do not speak of a *corps de théâtre*. We speak of *ensemble*[17] instead, "togetherness" as an alternative to authoritarian group arrangements. Ensemble theatre aspires to be devoid of the hierarchy of a star system, Brecht's Berliner Ensemble being a prototype of socialist society.[18] Form, content and creativity were interwoven (striated?) in a fabric (structure) of ethical values, each system of his Epic Theatre representing a piece in a dynamic ideological puzzle designed to stimulate the spectator's active engagement *via* dialectics. This revolutionary theatre demanded the collective commitment of all company members towards an expressly levelling agenda, where we might find something of the smooth being summoned too: in his clarion call to the proletarian artist, Brecht advocated that actors "be *Explorers* and teachers of the art of dealing with people. / Knowing their nature and demonstrating it you teach them / To deal with themselves. You teach them the great art / Of living together" (Brecht, 1976: 237, emphasis added).[19] The *ensemble*[20] like the *corps de ballet* is a collective noun that assumes the indivisibility of co-creators, individual humility towards the greater task binding different sensibilities and personalities. *Ensemble* and *corps* each connote communality and selflessness as humanizing forces in otherwise vertically organized structures. They depend on and reflect, in performative action, values of camaraderie and egalitarianism, codes of mutual respect, *an ethics of good practice*, a smoothing of the striated. With the politics of individualism, introduced by Thatcher in the UK 1980s and expanded on by contemporary popular culture, such collaborative processes are currently hard to foster and there is a patent fear among the younger generation of losing the opportunity to shine, succeed or even survive in large artistic organizations. We are certainly not all identical swans in a line. That is totalitarianism. So how do we orientate ourselves physically towards an alternative: a creative practice that is *felt*?[21]

There are various ways to educate the performer, according to cultural purpose. Presences, energies, sizes, genders, ethnicities, ages, abilities, traits and character are just some of the human material we engage with in making theatre. We can consciously train not to eradicate our differences but to elaborate creatively and collaboratively from them. No training is value-free. Any performer system embodies values. Whether it is the 5 a.m. start of a Kathakali apprentice, the daily barre work of the ballet dancer, the cleaning of the *dojo* before Aikido practice or the self-directed freedom of a Contact Improvisation *Jam,*[22] the context, environment and content of any training session will connote the form's assumptions about power as well as its relationship to rigour, effort, perfection and experience on the part of the trainee:

> [concern] is that the pure essence of Aikido, unadulterated by competitive egos, either personal or national, be kept firmly at the center of training and practice. After all *dojo*, "the place of enlightenment", is a word derived from the Sanskrit *bodhimanda,* the place where the ego self undergoes transformation into the egoless self. (Ueshiba, 1984: 10)

Spaces and places for learning inform our movement. If we move away from the striated straight lines of the ballet class how then might we defragment our bodies, experience them in smooth space inside and out? How can we address the feeling of being "out of touch"?[23] How to *move well*, physiologically and ethically?

T'ai Chi Ch'uan

T'ai chi ch'uan ("supreme ultimate boxing") is a soft internal martial art, practised individually. The form (there are many styles within its overarching set of principles) is a movement meditation, extremely detailed, embodying principles of Yin and Yang: "Every movement is circular and out of each motion comes its opposite" (Horwitz & Kimmelman, 1976: 29). T'ai chi uses animal metaphors and images– bird, snake, monkey and tiger – to reflect the human condition and the body in motion according to the principles: for example, the Tiger is actually the enemy within that must be overcome and embraced so as to achieve equilibrium. Equilibrium is physically practised so as to achieve a tranquil mental condition, but, as the form teaches, it is impossible to divide the mind from the body. Like many martial arts, the form teaches us to locate our "centre" deep in our pelvis, from whence energy springs. To work from this centre requires a gravitational dropping downwards of the whole body. This roots us into the floor, earths us though our feet. The body in this schema is in profound contrast to the headstrong heavenward Western classical ideal and brings to mind Bakhtin's heavy, earthy, all-inclusive body.

Push Hands is a training practice studied on its own or as part of a study of the form. The activity involves two partners moving together improvisationally through contact at the hand and wrist. The continuous sharing of balanced touch in repetitive movements, yielding to push as well as pushing, giving and receiving of direction, works to undo the natural instinct to resist force with force and block energy flow. Push Hands is an experiential way of reading your partner and developing sensitivity towards the direction and force of their intention. Nobody leads and nobody follows because each are involved in a continuum of exchange of forces. This requires profound "listening power" – responsive attention to the partner and the ability to balance the active and passive body–mind state so that the whole living system of both is in a state of reciprocity. It provides clear and instant feedback into the willfulness (or not) and ego of the practitioner, their ability to yield as well as initiate, their openness towards each other. "Despite being called Push Hands (tuishou)" says my teacher, Kinthissa, "when one comes in contact with a skilled practicant, one notices there is neither push nor a hand to push. Their body is together – posturally and energetically – one can find no edge, and their every movement embraces and envelops one in *boundlessness*" (Kinthissa, 2010, emphasis added). That word "boundless" again.

Profound ethics lie within this act of mutual touch: the opponent is not a force to be confronted with an equally opposing force thereby creating immovable and obstructive energy, but a partner to move *with – boundlessly* (Bakhtin, Deleuze and Guattari). Moving-with is, simplistically, the opposite of moving-against. It requires respect, attention and complicity. To be effective it requires balancing active and passive forces, accepting that both are necessary in a continual shift of relationship and that consequently there is no absolute control possible from either party. Push Hands could be considered a model of democratic consciousness, or at least, an improved model of conflict resolution, of negotiation *in action*.[24]

Aikido

> [Aikido] requires an ethical intention. A man must sincerely desire to defend himself without hurting others . . . The practice of the art of Aikido then becomes a harmonious interaction between two or more people, fulfilling Master Ueshiba's intention via translation of the highest ethics of the East

> (and West as well) into vital and active modes of conduct. (Westbrook & Ratti, 1980: 34)

Whereas t'ai chi originated in China centuries ago, aikido was developed in Japan in the early part of the twentieth century by Morihei Ueshiba as a synthetic martial art to express his utopian vision of universal peace. Ueshiba spent over 20 years developing the form that received its official recognition and name in 1942. Aikido is a contact art. At its core is the philosophy of neutralizing rather than destroying the opponent by harmonizing with the oncoming force of the attack. Just as in t'ai chi, the key is to match the forces between two individuals. Aikido trains you to reflect the opponent's force (make contact with it), and instantly deflect this, using circular principles to move yourself away from the attack and compel the attacker to "fall with their own energy". The attacker tumbles according to the force that they bring to the attack move. A straight line transforms into a curve.

Fig. 4-1. Ethics of defence in combat: illustration by O. Ratti from *Aikido and the Dynamic Sphere,* reproduced with kind permission from Adele Westbrook. Note that in panel A, B and C all the results are that a man is killed, whereas in panel D we have the "ethical self-defence" of aikido.

Partners act as a mutual instant-feedback system creating a "pathway of least resistance" so as to redirect the force of attack forwards and downwards into the floor. Aikido, like t'ai chi, is a practice of non-violence, of harmonizing opposites, of yielding to force within models of conflict.

Like Push Hands, hand-to-hand touch is the conduit of information. Unlike Push Hands (but more akin to the forms of t'ai chi itself) aikido training involves precise sequences of attack and defence actions that lead to falls and rolls. Working with bodily contact in an extremely detailed way, according to a set of rehearsed moves, a typical practice is rigorous and formal, with an emphasis on kinaesthetic communication over and above the verbal. You learn by repetition of moves, building flexibility and stamina and a confident relationship with the floor (normally a very thick mat). The *dojo* is a place where ritual and etiquette must be observed; this is a highly ethical environment, disciplined, respectful and concentrated.

Contact Improvisation (CI): Falling Together

Steve Paxton studied t'ai chi and aikido in the early 1970s at the same time as he researched and experimented with other pioneering postmodern dancers at Judson Church in New York. In 1972, his interest in the falls of aikido, where the body doesn't crash perpendicular to the ground but curves and rolls into it, led to the first experiment in what became known as Contact Improvisation. In a piece *Magnesium*, at Oberlin College, Ohio, Paxton worked with a group of men, training them in dance techniques and introducing them to the principles of the solo he had been working on in which he was exploring the idea of leaving the ground without planning the landing.

> I'd been working on a solo that had come out of Aikido dreams . . . I just wanted to leave the planet and not worry about the re-entry . . . to somehow have the skills to come back down without damage. (Paxton, 2008)

This single experiment, in the context of a fertile period of artistic iconoclasm, proved catalytic and rapidly developed into what is surely the most significant accelerated contribution to the development of movement and dance we have known. Paxton applied to his research not only the physical science of aikido, but its ethics: respect for your partner, opening and listening to the play of forces between you, reflecting rather than overpowering the other by force, harmonizing opposites. Such (anti-capitalist, anti-militaristic, anti-sexist) values ripple with meaning within and beyond the activity itself, expressed in many of its aspects: in CI the social connotations of gender and sexuality can be neutralized as in practice we ignore the hierarchy of body parts ("touchable" and "untouchable" zones) so the body becomes instead all-surface and all-information. Study of the physics of mass, movement, momentum and inertia produces a practice in which not only do women learn to support men physically without effort and damage but in which the representational and presentational traditions associated with men–women partnerships even of contemporary dance are erased in constant "circularity of space". As with aikido and its emphasis on curving and conditioning the body into circular positions for forward rolling, CI uses gravity and the actual weight of the body rather than stretching and reaching away from Nature into stylized lines as in dance techniques. The body folds, falls, lifts, levers, sticks, rolls, presses, leaps and plays with the partner's body in a constant state of listening (cf Push Hands and aikido) and attention to the information being transmitted at the ever-shifting point of contact. Intercorporaeity here is not social, emotional or erotic (though emotions can arise), but touch as information-imparting, clue-giving, opportunity-suggesting sensation. The touch of CI is directional. *Via* skin, into muscles and bone, sometimes skimming and sometimes deep, contact between movers follows "the pathway of least resistance" to find all the possibilities that reside in any fleeting second of human action in its surroundings. In CI we experience the world haptically in new ways, we blend with the world like Bakhtin's "unfinished" bodies and in utter contrast to the ballet dancer's "finished" image. And we make it up as we go along.

It's not all sweetness and light. In learning to yield we are balancing opposites, playing with ratios of yin and yang. At times effort and will are essential to push the movers into new dynamics where otherwise, over-submission might become repetitively touchy-feely.[25] As you become skilled in the fundamental principles of CI you learn to be pro-active without being domineering, to initiate without taking total control of or overpowering the other. In essence, and palpably, you take care of your partner and yourself. Attention to detail and a sense of what will and won't harm the body become imperative when working at speed and athletically. Physical risks are taken. Losing concentration, ignoring the other's needs, is not only selfish but also potentially dangerous. Thus many of the "fundamentals" – exercises that introduce CI players to managing their body weight, gravity, reconditioning reflexes, experimentation with falling, disorientation and the touch experience itself – including learning to recognize ways to protect and survive whilst opening up to the unpredictability of the interplay. Therein lies its rigour.

CI is studied in a random ordering of space (smooth) in contrast to the rectilinear (e.g. barres around the walls and lines of classical and contemporary dance classes). We don't use mirrors for visual auto-correction, and there is no "front". Alongside its mobile, unpredictable, variable dissemination in "smooth" spaces, the form has also infiltrated academies, more slowly but influencing movement education. Where its critics might find it boring, non-narrative and soggily "new age", its advocates comprehend its profundities from within, for above all, CI has always been rooted in a deep enquiry that has reflected and expanded on values outside of and against mainstream culture, describing alternatives *in motion*:

> It relies on the good sense of the body, not on mental will. CI happens in a condition in which the habitual and acculturated self is re-ordered from normal Western social conditioning. It is a natural event, first occurring in mother–child bonding, deriving from the prolonged ride in the womb which prenatal babies experience. Once born it continues to be a vehicle of communication between the infant and parents. Touch, the communication before verbal communication. Touch, a communication exiled as soon as there are other means. Touch, a communication which communicates the properties of the physical world to our bodies. Touch, which can be reclaimed as communication between people when they have some notion of choices they can make, free of cant and dogma, free of insinuation. CI, an art-sport which takes place in public, providing exercise and intimacy instead of sexercise and sintamacy (Paxton, 2010).

CI remains an overarching research question about the body's relationship to physical principles concentrated into myriad smaller, precise, phenomenological enquiries approached with an over-riding sense of play. Aside from other movement forms, practitioners have brought information from a range of other disciplines to bear on its development and application including psychotherapy, psychology, child-development, pedagogy, healing arts, sociology, anthropology and philosophy, whilst neuroscience opens possibilities for key new reflection and investigation.

Groping Towards a Conclusion

Touch is not sensation alone but encompasses and includes a vital and eloquent social and metaphorical dimension (Paterson, Paxton, Stewart, Turner, Grosz, Deleuze and Guattari *et al*). That doesn't mean we move metaphorically nor that we need to express metaphors in how we move, but, instead, we practise and research pragmatically, *physically* with appropriate attention. The rest follows. All the above movement disciplines involve physical contact between two or more partners. Each of them is studied primarily haptically. We work physically, inquisitively, experimentally, asking with our bodies "what happens if?" Such questions are rooted in the experience of the body itself *as it moves*. There is nothing to express outside of the studio beyond the phenomena of the event. We are not *representing* anything; there is no mimesis, no narrative to tell, no simpering love stories, no heroics (Rainer, 1968). We are not *expressing* emotions nor *describing* social roles (they are inscribed in us, waiting to be erased, redrawn). We are, rather, *being* "free of cant and dogma", free of the pressures that may be exerted on us in daily life, the domestic and professional roles we might occupy, the responsibilities, the stresses. CI unites the body with itself, equalizes our normally social-sexual significant parts with the body's entire organism. We become, instead, totally surface – but with depths – a canvas, clay, live raw material, a *felt* (sic). Experiencing touch illuminates a whole physics of movement, our bodies learning to recondition responses to the world – for purpose. We learn to take care of others, to work with good, kind touch and explore, amongst other things, all that might be useful in regressing to our crawling, rocking, rolling, embracing and *tactile origins*. Our judgements are appropriate to the task in hand. They are not the scrutinies or classifications traditionally associated with the distancing sense of sight we find in classical, spectatorial consumer-oriented art.

CI is close-up work, "nomadic", "infinite, open, and unlimited" (Deleuze & Guattari, 2008: 528). It suggests a re-invention of values – about dance and beauty, about bodies and differences, about what creativity and art practice can be, about our nature and our organic mysteries. And if we are living in increasingly "out of touch times" whilst paradoxically "hungering for touch" as Classen (2005) suggests, perhaps antidotes such as this ludic yet deep "art-sport" go some way to satisfy this basic need.

CI emerged at a particular moment of American political struggles of all kinds, and the counter-cultural values of its early quest are marked in its preoccupations. Whilst updating these ideas and their contemporary relevance is an ongoing project for CI's originators and subsequent generations – in the theoretical context of a burgeoning post-Foucaultian literature on the body and its meanings – the practice has endured the test of time as the form has also been appropriated, customized and absorbed into a broad curriculum of performer training and dramaturgy internationally.

Movement practices cannot be dissociated from their contexts, historical and social. CI, related ensemble work and the martial arts from which these derive invite our sense of social self to shift as our (primarily) haptic sense apparatus grows. The private experience of the studio moves out into the wider culture for, as Bryan Turner has stated unequivocally: "The critique of the text of the body therefore leads into critique of power relations within society" (Turner, 2001: 27). From touch, in this trajectory, it is possible to practise role-play and to train – a different model of human relationship, power roles and habituated behavioural patterns to carry into theatre as in life with which to communicate meanings beyond the physiologically driven solipsistic enquiry of practice-in-action. "The form itself seems to embody metaphors for abstract social relations, bringing the spectator's moral sense into play along with the bodies' (Banes & Alexander, 1980: 68). The French expression "être bien dans sa peau" literally translates as "being well in one's skin". Figuratively this means not only physical but psychological well-being, a sense of *feeling right;* and here I submit from experience that we might *feel right* (in all senses of the verb) if we admit that we belong close to the earth, our bodies "open" and "unfinished" rather than striving to escape our mortality in histrionic symbolic gestures of flight. This tangible discovery, revealed through physical activity and the whole apparatus of embodied perception and conscious awareness, can be psychophysically liberating as well as providing a strong foundation for original performance making. Meanwhile, practising non-violent martial arts when the arms race is accelerating and the media bombard us daily with images of bloodied and mutilated war victims, plus close, non-sexually-loaded flesh-to-flesh encounter when the commodification of sex is obsessional – "eyes are awash with it many times a day" (Paxton, 2010) – suggests the possibility of at least glimpsing, and touching, another model for finding ourselves as respectful, interactive beings in an embodied and mutual space.

"Movement" has many meanings, each of which implies motion and transformation: a body moves in space; collective human effort strives to bring about political and cultural change. Within the frames discussed above, touch plainly constitutes a radical social critique in-action, indicating how in effect and affect, we are able to re-write ourselves differently in that space and time between "what is and ought to be" to engage actively in expressing, experiencing and challenging social values and hierarchies. It is this that makes the touch sense such a particularly socializing, adapting and public medium through which we might, as a consequence of feeling better in our skins, find ourselves able to overcome alienation and begin to move – and be moved – towards finding forms and models for those possibilities of continuous, creative, transformation designated as "good", or at the very least better than those that history has prescribed.

Notes

1 *Alan Read* – It might be no coincidence that Alan Read, Professor of Drama, Theatre and Performance Studies in the Department of English at Kings College, University of London, worked at Dartington College of Arts in the 1980s at the same time as pioneering postmodern dancer-choreographers Mary Fulkerson and Steve Paxton from the USA were disseminating the idea and practice of postmodern dance to the theatre students there, many of whom spread such ideas in the UK and beyond in the development of their own practice.

2 Merleau-Ponty has been criticized by feminists for his generalizations on subjectivity. He takes his (white male etc) position as a norm. Grosz (1994; cf. Turner, 2001) argues that whilst he crucially leaves out questions of sexual difference, the fact that he explicitly attempts to integrate the Cartesian duality of mind and body and bring perception to the forefront in this does offer feminist theory some useful critical strategies.

3 The word 'haptic' derives from the Greek *haptesthai* and refers to the somatic sense and sensation of touch. Haptics are rooted in three physical senses: proprioception (self-awareness of the body *in space,* as present, in flesh, muscle, bone), kinaesthesia (the sense of movement) and the vestibular (relating to the sense of balance controlled by the vestibular system of the inner ear). Whilst *haptics* as applied to art, psychology, engineering and digital technologies embraces the idea of touch as operating at a deeper level than the cutaneous surface of the skin (Paterson, 2007), the term itself doesn't encompass the wider social, imaginative, social, political and cultural meanings of touch, the "all of culture" that Classen is addressing. I am suggesting that by working with touch as movement praxis we might reconcile the somatic with the cultural – consciously – if we choose.

4 Though of course deceptive touch is the professional province of e.g. the actor, the wrestler and the prostitute.

5 Arguably, still the case in a technological age, even if this "stuff" is a keyboard in a call centre.

6 Literally "earth-to-earth", a term in classical ballet describing movement that is close to the ground, without effort at elevation.

7 *Aesthesis* is the Greek word for perception. As a philosophy (of art) it involves exploring states of mind and response mechanisms to manifestations of beauty. Aristotle's concept of aesthesis was of a sensory faculty that is affected /altered by the impression made on the receiver, including emotional affect (Paterson, 2007: 80–81).

8 The pun is deliberate. The heart here refers to a site of emotional excitement, *feeling.*

9 The language of wounds and broken flesh: pain wakes us up, shakes us up. We all love a good cry, a good tear-washed catharsis. This is the stuff of tragedy. But we can also be touched deeply without suffering. We can laugh instead, or gently smile in recognition. We can be tickled, stroked or nudged without this cruelty of *punctum.* We might just feel *connected* to each other/the world/the artist by experiencing disarmament in the face of a work of art. He is speaking of images and words as having a direct impact on the human imagination and soul (*aesthetic* responses).

10 At the Anish Kapoor exhibition, Royal Academy, London 2009, cheerful guards repeatedly prevented visitors from giving in to the temptation to touch the huge train of vermillion wax pushing through the doors of the galleries. Many of the thwarted (myself included) sought spattered traces of this gorgeous crimson substance at either end of the tracks and stole these fleshy pieces to test between our eager fingers.
11 As Classen (2005) also comments, stigmatization of touch in the contemporary museum excludes the sight-impaired.
12 The magician/conjuror invites tactile verification: "feel it, it really is hollow, empty, solid, real, isn't it?!" etc. *Feel it for yourself.* Touch affirms perception, especially where there is doubt. "Doubting Thomas" in the Bible needed to touch Christ's wounds as proof of his resurrection, whilst Mary Magdalene was instructed by Christ to trust her eyes, her gnosis: *noli mi tangere* (do not touch me) perhaps being less of an order than an invitation to believe in him, and herself.
13 *The Thinking Body: A Study of the Balancing Forces of Dynamic Man* (first published in 1937), is the title of the influential book referred to and applied by many postmodern/new dance practitioners.
14 Interestingly, echoing this argument that will draw on certain Asian martial arts and their influence on a branch of contemporary Western movement, the authors offer two versions of ancient board games that represent martial tactics: chess (a game of military tactic against identifiable characters) belongs to the striated, whereas the game of Go (based in territory and capture, played on a board with non-figurative pieces) belongs to the smooth. Chess is more rational, Go more intuitive, though both require strategy.
15 Perhaps he/she is the "flaneur", bohemian, the one who thinks laterally and not vertically, the artist.
16 The performance artist Raimond Hoghe (http://www.raimundhoghe.com/en/en_disturbances.html) calls one of his solos and a lecture by this title (quoting Pier-Paulo Pasolini); see Johnson, 2005.
17 Actually far more egalitarian versions of ensemble and group theatre emerged in the 1960s and 1970s. Feminist, leftist theatres often did without a director at all.
18 Though let's not forget that it was Stanislavski, again, who wrote that "In spite of my great admiration for individual splendid talents I do not accept the star system. Collective creative effort is the root of our kind of art. That requires ensemble acting and whoever mars that ensemble is committing a crime not only against his comrades but also against the very art of which he is the servant" (1988: 257).
19 The explorer is perhaps akin to the nomad, at least certainly moving away from fixed knowledge and, supposedly, towards new discoveries, however didactic Brecht's intentions (especially with the *Lehrstucke*, "learning plays").
20 Like jazz musicians, practitioners familiar with the form meet at appointed times and practice the improvisation form without directors or leaders. This has been part of the CI (sub)culture internationally for some decades and has helped the form to spread and flourish in communities of dance/theatre and non-professional enthusiasts.
21 For all this importance of human tactility as a way of experiencing and interpreting our relationship to habitat and humans, urban culture – pre and post digital

– nonetheless remains primarily visual, city life being a round-the-clock optical assault. Bombarding us with erotically charged lures to the bliss of tactile gratification in anything from cat food to bubble bath, the adman's repertoire of pleasure's appearance proves to be a chimera, a striptease shimmying up to our eyes yet forbidding any tactile engagement. This is complicated further by the indirect touch of fingertip tactility involved in producing on our computer screens – daily for an ever increasing number of the world's population – the same breed of chimerical images. If actual touch is promised whilst the imagery denies our actually *feeling* anything, Classen (2005) suggests, touch may paradoxically be currently the "hungriest sense of postmodernity" and the disjuncture between the constant suggestion of tactility and our actual deprivation of this might account for a contemporary sense of alienation and of "being out of touch" with our environment.

22 T'ai chi principles are thought to have originated in the twelfth century, though the first style emerged from the Chen family in the sixteenth century. The links to the form with Neo-Confucianism (that synthesizes Taoist and Buddhist thinking) seem evident in the form but the exact lineage of ideas in relation to the evolution of its form and styles remains a source of scholarly debate. What remains clear in the practice is that respect for Nature, the balancing of forces, the neutralizing of attacks, and a lucid, calm relationship to self and other suggests, like many other martial arts, that the way of the warrior is not to destroy and kill but to seek a peaceful good life.

23 Whilst the conscious mind struggles, not always successfully, to maintain distinction from the body and its senses, for intellectual control through reason alone, the English language includes telling tropes of touch, some of which relate specifically to mental processes – "to grasp", "to touch on", "to seize", "to grapple with", "to chew over", "to wrestle with", "to cleave to" – suggesting an abiding association between mind, body and feeling (Classen, 2005; Montagu, 1978). Meanwhile actual touch in a social and cultural sense suggests too much body and not enough mind and so, linguistically, we will also find touch and feeling demeaned in the term "touchy-feely", implying lack of intellectual rigour and sensual self-indulgence in the tactile event. "Touchy-feely" connotes close proximity.

24 Whilst "art-sport" is an apt term for some of its actual rules-of-the-game and CI practitioners do certainly "play" the form, it can in no way encapsulate the enormous global impact the form has had on contemporary choreography and dance-theatre/physical theatre. CI has entered the dance consciousness in a highly influential way through the vocabulary of physical training because internationally practitioners have been invited to teach students the form, in both freelance and college contexts. CI was introduced to the UK by American dancer Mary Fulkerson when teaching at Dartington College of Arts from 1973. A whole generation of post-Dartington dance-theatre artists have emerged in the UK since, who have taken the form into their work on stage and continued to spread the practice in their teaching. CI is now on many curricula even outside of dance schools.

25 The principles of contact can be applied to prosthetics. Bamboo possesses particular qualities as a natural material that we can use as a metaphor for the kind of ideal physical condition/quality that enables us to "unblock" and

release energies and move with deeply relaxed attention and true power. We can move *like bamboo*, imagining its properties to help us find that yielding yet present state of action. We can also bring bamboo sticks themselves into the pragmatics of training, learning to dilate our physical energy through them. Bamboo is hollow between its nodules and this tube, usually with a tapered tip, conducts the energy of the person holding it. Many exercises can be derived from this as a contact game. In tip-to-tip contact, the energy of each player will travel right through the stick and be palpably experienced by the partner. Such contact produces magical circling of the two sticks, or simply their rising off the floor. You can work with throwing games, rhythm and passing. You can apply tip-to-tip contact in a circle in a group. You can play with the stick around your partner's body (without touching) to awaken their reflexes. You can hold one stick between two people with the lightest of central palm contact and move together through space, extending your awareness of the exchange of energy by ducking and diving together around other playing pairs. And so on. Bamboo stick work appropriates and plays with principles found in t'ai chi, aikido and Contact Improvisation. I first witnessed this work at Peter Brook's *Centre Internationale de Recherches Théâtrales* in Paris in 1971. His actors were working with actors from the American deaf theatre, exploring the power of non-verbal communication. The director Andrej Serban, among others including myself, uses bamboo as a training tool (Serban, 1999).

References

Bachelard, Gaston. 1994. *The Poetics of Space.* MA. Beacon Press.

Bakhtin, Mikhail. 1984. *Rabelais and his World.* Translated by Helene Iswolsky. Bloomington, IN. Indiana University Press.

Banes, Sally, and Alexander, R. 1980. 'Steve Paxton: Physical Things', in *Terpsichore in Sneakers: Post-Modern Dance.* Boston. Houghton Mifflin.

Barthes, Roland. 1981. *Camera Lucida: Reflections On Photography.* New York. Hill and Wang.

Brecht, Bertold. 1976. *Brecht: Poems Part Two 1929–1938.* London. Eyre Methuen

Cixous, Helene, and Clement, Catherine. 1986. *The Newly Born Woman (La Jeune Nee).* Translated by Betty Wing. London and Minneappolis. University of Minnesota Press.

Classen, Constance. 2005. *The Book of Touch.* Oxford and New York. .

Deleuze, Giles, and Guattari, Felix. 2008. *A Thousand Plateaus: Capitalism and Schizophrenia.* London and New York. Continuum.

Foster, Susan Leigh. 1996. *Corporealities: Dancing Knowledge, Culture and Power.* London and New York. Routledge.

Foucault, Michel. 1991. *Discipline and Punish: The Birth of the Prison.* Harmondsworth. Penguin.

Grosz, Elizabeth *Volatile Bodies* Indiana University Press, Indiana 1994

Hockney, David. *A Day On the Grand Canal with The Emperor of China: Or Surface Is Illusion But So Is Depth.* [Motion picture.] Produced & directed by

Philip Haas. New Yorker Films.
Horwitz, Tem, and Kimmelman, Susan. 1976. *Tai Chi Chuan: The Technique of Power.* Chicago. Chicago Review Press.
Howes, David (ed.). 2006. *The Empire of the Senses: The Sensual Culture Reader.* Oxford and New York. Berg.
Kinthissa. 2010. Private correspondence with Anna Furse, 14 January.
Merleau-Ponty, Maurice. 2004. *The Phenomenology of Perception.* London. Routledge and Kegan Paul.
Money, Keith. 1965. *The Art of Margot Fonteyn.* London. Michael Joseph.
Montagu, Ashley; *Touching: The Human Significance of the Skin*, Harper & Row (New York) 1978.
Paterson, Mark. 2007. *The Sense of Touch: Haptics, Affects and Technologies.* Oxford and New York. Berg.
Paxton, Steve. 1987. *Fall After Newton.* [Video.] Videoda. http://www.artsalive.ca/en/dan/mediatheque/videos/videosDetails.asp? mediaID=428
Paxton, Steve. 2008. *Steve Paxton Discusses First Contact Improv Work.* [Video.] http://greatdance.com/videos/2008/08/steve-paxton-discusses-first-c/
Paxton, Steve. 2010. Private correspondence with Anna Furse, 4th January.
Rainer, Yvonne. 1968. Statement accompanying *The Mind is a Muscle.* http://mitpress.mit.edu/catalog/item/default.asp?ttype=2&tid=11290.
Read, Alan. 1995. *Theatre and Everyday Life: An Ethics of Performance.* London and New York. Routledge.
Serban, Andre. 1999. *The Use of Sticks in Performance Training.* [Video.] Exeter. Arts Archives. http://www.arts/archives.org/cat19.htm
Stanislavski, Constantin. 1988. 'Toward an Ethics for the Theatre', in *Building a Character* trans. Elizabeth Reynolds Hapgood. London. Eyre Methuen.
Todd, Mabel Elsworth. 1997. *The Thinking Body: A Study of the Balancing Forces of Dynamic Man.* London. Dance Books.
Turner, Bryan S. 2001. *The Body and Society.* London and New Delhi. Sage Publications.
Ueshiba, Kisshomaru. 1984. *The Spirit of Aikido.* Tokyo, San Francisco and New York. Kodansha International.
Westbrook, Adele, and Ratti, Oscar. 1980. *Aikido and the Dynamic Sphere.* Vermont and Tokyo. Tuttle.
Young, Iris Marion. 1990. *Throwing Like a Girl and Other Essays in Feminist Philosophy and Social Theory.* Bloomington, IN. Indiana State University Press.

5

CRISIS

Simon Bayly

For a school half-term family holiday to the Cornish coast in England in 2006, without really understanding the set-up, we had booked into a converted farm that turned out to be regularly used as a holiday retreat for a dozen or so extended families with children aged from 2 to around 16. These families return to the place every year, with some parents continuing a tradition they entered themselves as children decades earlier. For this kind of English holiday destination, though fairly homogenous in comparison to the typical metropolitan mix of ethnicities, this is a very mixed bunch in terms of class, economic and professional backgrounds. In conversation with the families, it was clear that they appreciate its rough and ready simplicity and the opportunity to temporarily gather as a community of sorts who, on the face of it, have very little in common. However, this history appeared to be drawing to a close. The owners of the farm, then in their seventies and needing to downscale, were planning to sell it off piecemeal at market rates, with regular visitors getting first call. Given Cornwall's rising status as the second-home location of choice for the affluent from elsewhere in the country, very few of the families visiting that week could even contemplate the gigantic sums involved and so faced the loss of this amenity.

As we soon discovered, the tradition of a play written, directed and performed entirely by the children during the regular May half-term break has been informally established. The teenagers come up with an idea and write a script using email during the spring and everything else is sorted out on site during the holiday week itself. As a theatre-maker and neophyte theatre studies academic myself, I was both fascinated and disconcerted by the possibility of being drawn into the intimacies and intrigues of the final preparations, perhaps in the same way that every medical practitioner must feel on hearing the call "Is there is doctor in the house?" However, to their credit, the producing collective took no interest at all in the appearance of a so-called professional in their midst. For their production in 2006, the players had chosen to adapt the tale of the Three Little Pigs into a new version entitled *The Three Little Chavs.*[1] While, on reflection, it might not be such a stretch from the stereotypical anthropomorphisms of the "pig" to those of the "chav", my expectation was of a not so subtle and not so funny performance of social prejudice, to which our eldest son, aged 8, had been co-opted as backstage hand and general hanger-about. Over the week, in between surfing in the pouring rain, he would disappear for various rehearsals and was typically less than forthcoming about what went on in them.

The venue chosen specifically for this production, in this beautiful seaside spot with many picturesque site-specific possibilities (including a large abandoned stone quarry that many a professional would surely have regarded as a gift), is a bleak, empty, concrete-floored garage. The rain has stayed away and the show is scheduled to start around 4 p.m. The audience assemble in front of the garage on bring-your-own seating, younger kids squatting at the front, so close they are almost in the garage, adults towards the rear, accompanied by large quantities of wine, beer, crisps and fizzy drinks. The set consists of a few pieces of discarded building materials and grubby chairs. Casting, costuming and performance style draw on an era of British Christmas pantomime that the cast could not logically have witnessed themselves, featuring botched cross-dressing, balloon breasts, big sunglasses and barely comprehensible dialogue. Some performers read their lines off bits of paper, others have partially learned them verbatim, exits and entrances are purely tokenistic, almost sarcastic, as if everyone is just a stand-in for a lazy but "proper" someone else who never bothered to show up, the familiar stock-in-trade techniques of the contemporary post-professional actor in Western "experimental" performance traditions. These non-performers "corpse", dry up, trip and knock things over, miss all manner of beats, but without the slightest sense of shame, embarrassment or concern. In fact, their prime affect is a generous, confident indifference. But this not a studied casualness, rather a type of detachment that might pass as "philosophical". What has to be done, has to be done. We just have to do this, get through it, taking as long as it takes, with as many mistakes as may come along. Who cares? Who's really watching anyway? We don't mind and we know you don't mind either. Spectators of all ages continue their own conversations; some wander off completely into the surrounding gardens or into the cottages for some more glasses.

However, the adapted plot is utterly transparent in its ruthless Brechtian simplicity: single Mother Chav cannot cope with her recalcitrant three little chavs in her owner-occupied council flat, so throws them out to make their own way. Alone in her home, she becomes depressed and suicidal. The Wolf, rebranded as a gang leader-cum-property developer with paedophiliac tendencies, is aided by a curiously upper class council worker now seeking to permanently separate Mother Chav from her children on grounds of neglect. Playing on her financial and emotional weakness, they persuade her to sell the flat – a placard reads "Chav-ville" – under a 1980s-style government incentive scheme, but for a miserable sum, effectively leaving her homeless. However, the separated chav children discover the plot, and with the aid of a neighbour-cum-fairy-godmother, join forces and take violent revenge on the Wolf, reclaim their familial home and are reunited with their mother. The end. Sweets are thrown to the audience, the younger spectators fight in the mud to collect them.

Naturally, other parents wielded digital cameras and video recorders as an integral part of their spectatorship. I don't like to take photographs in any situation, but attending this performance all I could do was photograph, borrowing my son's camera and surreptitiously wandering around the perimeter of the audience, as if attempting to record some archaic form of soon-to-be-extinct ritual. The performance was equally compelling and repelling in its systematic invocation and dereliction of theatrical conventions, both mainstream and avant-garde, and is equal in my memory now to only two or three other performance events I have encountered. And to cope with that ambivalence, I went to work on documenting it – here was some interesting material that I could hopefully make use of, without really understanding why, just as it felt impossible for me to engage with *The Three Little Chavs* as the kind of spectator I am used to being. Of course, to perform as a pseudo-ethnographic image-maker is a particularly affected performance of spectatorship – perhaps the perfect embodiment of what the Italian philosopher Giorgio Agamben has described as the spectator with taste, who is confronted with:

> something that, as it seems to him, puts him back in contact with his innermost truth, yet he cannot identify with it. The spectator's is the most radical split: his principle is what is most alien to him; his essence is in that which, by definition, does not belong to him. Taste, in order fully to be, has to become separate from the principle of creation; but without genius, taste becomes a pure reversal, that is, the very principle of perversion. (Agamben 1999: 16)

If we can substitute an eighteenth-century notion of taste for the twenty-first-century notion of an educated critical awareness, such as might result from a disciplined study of performance, then spectators who literally trade on the value of their critical awareness would appear to be in a compromising position. This is indeed the case in relation – or rather in non-relation – to the performance just described, which would seem profoundly problematic as an example to offer up for intellectual scrutiny. Accepting Agamben's thesis, the trouble is all too evident – "how to spectate" (without the genius reserved for the principle of creation) – yet without enacting the very principle of perversion, which aims to assimilate the other to its own form of enjoyment. But isn't the very principle of performance precisely an invitation to do exactly that, to produce and partake in collective forms of enjoyment, however that ambivalent term might be understood?

A performance that is neither solicited nor anticipated recruits such a perverse spectator. This figure is then confronted with its own law of desire:

in this instance, an encounter with a boundaried collective of sorts rehearsing its own unbinding, non-relation, non-identity, non-belonging via a collective theatrical "ritual", whose very lack of efficacy and entertainment is so clearly the public secret that is both efficacious and entertaining, shared by everyone in its social setting. That idea might be otherwise articulated, say, by describing how this performance had so efficiently embodied the social and economic contradictions of its own situation and grasped the centrality of class, family and property to those same contradictions. Or how it functioned as an ironic theatrical act of mourning for the anticipated dissolution of a rare occurrence of a small, self-organizing, non-kinship-based pseudo-community, brutally passed off without a trace of melancholia as a throwaway skit barely worth the attention. Or, eschewing any sort of compromise with the cryptic culture of interpretation, this event might be better complemented by some performative writing that might get amongst its affects and effects more sensitively. Or to contribute to what Alan Read (reading Bruno Latour) has recently articulated as a "showciology", an improvised sociology that trades on appearances (theatrical or otherwise), through a description as a commonplace of the everyday rather than a privileged, special place of art, one practice amongst others that might be partaking in a modest "reassembly of the social", evidencing a cultural know-how well in control of its relation to the mixed cultural blessings of performance, rather than making any kind of direct claim for the political. This last possibility holds out the most hope, but as in Read's own writing in *Theatre, Intimacy and Everyday Life*, the marvellously prodigious and promiscuous thinking that departs from theatre finds itself piling anomalous example upon example (from cephalopod biology to Colin Powell at the UN to – and closest to my own example above – the school nativity play) in a series in which moments of theatre are but insubstantial sideshows which cannot detain the onrush of enthusiasm to expand the collective. But none of these possibilities appears viable or desirable, either at the time looking down on the event with a camera, or now, looking back at what I can't recall. What follows is simply a start at attempting to reckon with that moment of minor crisis, so often sutured to the condition of being mid-life, when current experience can neither be assimilated by prior understanding nor projected forward into a determinate future.

A similar crisis of dissociation, but more elegantly represented, seems to have befallen my colleague Joe Kelleher on a different occasion. Meditating on a work by the Spanish live artist La Ribot, he writes of the performers that "their world is not our world . . . their words, although they look so similar, are not our words . . . their laughter has nothing to do with us" and concludes that

> This is an illusion that might persuade us to add to the question "How to act?" a matching question "How to spectate?", if it really is the case that an effect of acting can be enough to separate us so radically from other people that even their most direct statements, their most explicit gestures, become indeterminate for us. (Kelleher 2008: 58)

But Kelleher has much to say about and in spite of this predicament, which in other renderings is profoundly symptomatic of the theatre's basic problem, recognized by a lineage of thinkers stretching back through Situationism to Rousseau and beyond. In this strain of thought, the theatre expresses a particular and perennial ethical problem, that of separation and its overcoming. If an ethos signifies a way of life held in common, a set of values and attitudes immanent to any particular social configuration, then the separation between spectator and actor, passivity and activity, is simply a bad thing. The theatre is unethical in its very constitution, sundering individuals from their collective being together, substituting hollow representations for living action, alienating so-called "subjects" from the means of emancipation from their ostensible subjection, dividing those who move, speak and act from those who sit and remain silent. The philosophical prejudices and prohibitions mounted against the spectacle from Plato to Debord are all united in their accusations against its unethical nature. In its turn, the theatre has turned this rejection and repression to its own critical advantage, returning everywhere as the repressed radicality of a performative paradigm and the advent of a generalized but critical theatricality that can help animate the sustained period of waiting that characterizes the thinking of the post-communist left in the current political era. Indeed, so familiar is this refrain that it is tempting to think that contemporary thinking would surely have found a way to move beyond this particular impasse. But this is an ethico-political-aesthetic dilemma that refuses to go away. For example, as Baz Kershaw plainly puts it in his recent thinking on a sense of immanent crisis that braids together ecologies of theatre and performance with other ecosystems:

> I have come to think that the production of spectators is the primary business of theatres, regardless of what is onstage, and that possibly in some respects, at least, such business is profoundly anti-ecological. In other words, spectatorship as such, even though there may be many versions of it, historically is probably a major part of the theatre's contribution to the environmental crisis. (Kershaw 2007: 5)

If, in the age of ecological catastrophism, producing spectators is still the basic problem of performance, then presumably the remedy to address the multitude of ethical and political ills that come with an addiction to spectating might still be, as it was for Plato and Rousseau, to transform actors and spectators into participants. This is evidenced in so-called "relational turn" that has followed swiftly on from the "ethical turn" in contemporary art practice, now receiving an ecological inflection through consideration of the human as inescapably in relation to the constraints and capacities of the biosphere.

However, neither Kershaw nor many others writing on theatre and performance would perhaps be fully prepared to embrace what Rousseau was prepared to countenance: the theatre's self-abolition in favour of art itself becoming immanent to an ecological aesthetics of collectivity in which "the good life" that art continually anticipates but also defers, finally comes to pass. This aestheticization of the body politic, freighted with the communitarian legacies of twentieth-century totalitarianism, has simply become untenable. (Unfortunately for both the theory and practice of leftist post-war politics, this has generated a widespread critical suspicion of any type of attempt at collective organization as inescapably repressive and/or exclusionary.) Thus the ethical life to come either requires a new art, art's perpetual self-cancellation, or both. This contemporary paradox of performance – that its aesthetic, ethical and political ambitions are both produced and deferred in an oscillation between art's absolute autonomy or its absolute dissolution into life – has been perhaps most effectively articulated by Jacques Rancière. In line with his arguments for the incalculable political effects of aesthetic procedures, Rancière also opposes any form of teaching based on the division between those in possession of knowledge and those deemed ignorant. Everyone and anyone can acquire whatever knowledge is useful for them in their own way, just as spectators can and must make their own out of whatever is presented to them, independent of any aesthetic prescription. Furthermore, the notion of a "critical" art, which seeks to directly connect the address of the art work either to a specific socio-political determination or to a discourse of the unrepresentable (and to correspondingly ethical courses of political action), has lost whatever purchase it had on the ideological configuration of modernity. Unlike in the early days of critique, a hard core of ideological reality no longer lurks behind the spectacle of appearances, awaiting its unveiling. Today, Rancière implies, everyone knows precisely in which ways he or she is oppressed or repressed: we are all virtuoso participants in the machinations of capital and spectacle. But unfortunately, this knowledge does not necessarily lead to either understanding or action, despite a century of politicized art practice that attempted to persuade its audiences otherwise. In fact, it is only by securing in advance the guilt, complicity and inaction of its willing audiences that "critical" art has been able to sustain itself in spite of the withering away of the wider social and political movements that gave rise to it in the first place.

While hostile to ethics as a zone of indistinctness that blurs the spheres of politics and aesthetics, Rancière nevertheless offers an implicitly ethical prescription for aesthetic practice, which can sketch new dissensual configurations of what can be seen and who can articulate it only on the paradoxical condition that it does not anticipate its meanings, affects or effects. Against Deleuze and with Kant, art must once again proceed to articulate the aesthetic as that "which is without any concept" and which advances only by retracing the shifting line that separates art from non-art, rather than seeking to cancel itself out in a merger with life (as via the succession of avant-gardes from Dada onwards) or by a retreat to the melancholy discourse of the unrepresentable within a generalized regime of "the state of exception" (Agamben), an ethics of alterity (Levinas, Derrida) or an aesthetic of the sublime (Lyotard), all which interminably await a new basis for society that is "to come". This preference for an art of engaging disengagement finds echoes in much contemporary writing on theatre, whose ethical and political potential may only emerge at the point at which it abandons ethics and politics (Ridout 2009, Kelleher 2009, Read 2008) in the more or less familiar formulations it has accrued to date.

What Rancière appears to demand of art is that it simply leaves the spectator to his or her own dissensual devices, in much the same way that the properly democratic teacher ought neither anticipate nor determine the necessary knowledges and desires of the student. In this axiomatic assumption of equality, all education is necessarily self-education, all emancipation is self-emancipation, which may or may not converge with the emancipatory projects of other selves. Truly aesthetic and political acts are thus acts of dis-identification which refuse all invitations to participate in pseudo-utopian experiences of participatory togetherness or synergetic co-presence of embodied minds bound together in an auto-poetic feedback loop. A similar autodidactic imperative would appear to underpin the impersonal formalism of Badiou's philosophical system, which has proved particularly amenable to a theatrical thinking. Perhaps the most important distinction in his thinking is that between an event and a situation – the local structure of a world as it appears, how it is, the way things are, variably organized by power, difference, opinion and knowledge. But, as Sam Gillespie suggests, this distinction might rest entirely on the ability of "a select number of human beings to recognise events" (Gillespie 2006: 165), processes that emerge out of a void in the situation to puncture in and initiate the advent of a truth construed as ethics of fidelity to the event itself. Gillespie has an intriguing recourse to Lacan, one of Badiou's few stated mentors, to explain the inescapably subjective and affect-laden dimension of events and the so-called truth procedures that arise from them. What seems important here is the ability to recognize that is critical, which implies a kind of subject-in-waiting who is set just to one side of an emergent event – a particular kind of spectator, possessed of a particular kind of educated sensibility or susceptibility that can detect this emergence. The event is a local collapse in the consistency of appearance, an unbinding of the relations between the elements of a situation. But, although axiomatically universal in its address, not everyone is necessarily able to respond. In this collapse, a very particular sort of "aristocratic" subject is born, phoenix-like and given over to the unpleasure of a non-relation in which the inherent inconsistency of the situation is exposed to the possibility of the new.

Part of a political rationale underlying a desire to study – and to teach – performance might well be to produce human beings who can recognize in the world the kind of event formally articulated in Badiou's philosophy and thus entertain the possibility of entering into a process of fidelity to it – or in other words, to get a life. But this type of pedagogical (relational) imperative is refused both by Badiou and Rancière. However important it might be in embodying an ethics of truths or a redistribution of the sensible, art cannot teach anyone any lessons, either through representational mediation or acts of ethical immediacy. As Peter Hallward points out, for Rancière, Badiou and many of their contemporaries, "relation itself often figures as essentially binding, irredeemably contaminated by mastery and the social 'weight' of domination" (Hallward, 2006: 18). From a theatrical perspective, this refusal of an aesthetics or politics based on any kind of primary relationality or dependency is a profoundly difficult challenge, given that the theatre is based on an axiomatic relation that is paradoxically materialized through the separation of actor and spectator, as well as the production, not just of the individual spectator, but of the public as audience. There are difficult questions here about the transmission and organization of knowledges, affects, sensibilities, convictions and decisions, about the new forms of being-in-common that even the relation of non-relation gestures towards.

Hence what faces the figure of the critical spectator, caught in something of a crisis when faced with the ethico-political art of non-relation, is not simply a paradox, but an enigma. A paradox is something that can be at least partially understood, its poles delineated, its movements mapped, as Rancière does with the paradoxes of "political" art. But what makes something an enigma is perhaps the extent to which all understanding slides off its impermeable surface, accessible only by an unfamiliar means belonging to a higher power. Enigmatic moments of art that are both literally and metaphorically opaque acquire particular significance for this type of spectator: the passing wave to a parent from his child in the school nativity play that turns out to be a leave-taking, rather than a greeting (Read, 2008: 123ff); the ill-humour of a performed laughter that has neither apparent cause nor object (Kelleher, 2008); the darkly illuminated limbs of a dancer arranged to disorganize the coherence of the human body (Ridout, 2009: 67–9); an artwork in which an illuminated text on the surface of a black box describes the unviewable photograph of atrocity that enclosed within it (Rancière, 2009: 95–7) or the much referenced "Auschwitz" scene in Societas Raffaello Sanzio's 1999 production, *Genesi*, in which white-costumed children undertake obscure actions behind several layers of white scrim. In all these examples, and others like them, the enigma is also a seduction (and nowhere more so than in the context of the palpable physical presences of performance), a thing of fascination, pleasure and promise whose origin and destination remain mysterious not only to the spectator, but also to the actor: an effectively enigmatic performance is one that does not know what it is doing and which is "eventalized" by one who does not know what to make of it.

What is critical here, and perhaps also something of a crisis (a moment of suspension or hesitation before a future that is severed from the past) is the fact that this enigma can no longer be pedagogically decoded – to mean this or that, or both this and that – but simply witnessed, evoked and described. Its workings are to be revealed, but the ultimate destination of its address left open to whatever might be made of it by anyone and everyone. The enigma manifests as a kind of unwilled non-sense that offers itself as both an affective experience of unknowing but also an opening to an alternative future that seemed to have been ruthlessly foreclosed by the representative powers of mimesis. What is perhaps even more problematic for the critical possibilities of spectatorial witnessing that can recognize the enigma as event is that a "good" witness, a properly ethical witness, is someone who neither chose to witness what they saw, nor can willingly offer testimony that is able to substitute for the witnessed event itself. Like the artwork itself, the spectator as witness who is obliged to speak of an experience in which "something happened" must refuse any easy or direct connection between perception, affection, signification and action. But he or she must somehow attest to the fact of something having happened that "confronts its spectators or participants with something radically other, something that could not be assimilated by their existing understanding" (Ridout 2009: 67). At the same time, the task is precisely not to assimilate it through an existing understanding of their own.

For Badiou, it is the task of philosophy itself to think together the eventful nature of its four separate conditions (science, love, politics and art). I would suggest that it is this kind of theatrically derived sense of spectatorship, the suffering of a non-relation, that has produced some of the most resonant thinking which sets out to reclaim the ethical or political specificity of the theatrical, even as it refuses previous iterations of the politics or ethics of the aesthetic. Put simply, thinking strictly through theatre, which is by no means limited to thinking about theatre, permits a thinking of the evental truth of non-relation.

But could it be that this thinking is, ultimately, restricted to such a truth by the primacy of the observer that conditions the theatrical experience, as appears to be the case for the encounter with performance with which I began? In a number of local discourses, thinking through theatre has gained a renewed prominence over and against a pervasive generalization of performance. From this perspective emerge a particular set of issues: participatory art practice is typically problematic, ineffective and manipulative; audience enjoyment of and engagement with these forms of manipulation is either frustrated, ideologically suspect or simply and unproductively embarrassing; theatre in particular, art in general, has no real leverage on the world and its lack of instrumentality is precisely its political point; "political theatre" as such is a category error, a well-intentioned but misguided renewal of an avant-garde tradition that has simply run aground on the shores of another episteme.[2] Obviously, these perspectives are not new and are highly contested, as much I suspect by those, including myself, who hold them as by anyone else. Yet it seems we are a long way from theatre as a place where what is made present is, for example, the public as an association of individuals gathered in their heterogeneous and democratic inconsistency, the insurrectionary power of an event, or a set of embodied minds reassembling the social in a utopian moment of engaged or estranged enthralment.

Or perhaps this is exactly what was happening in and around the performing garage in Cornwall that day, drifting into the undecidability of an English spring afternoon, in some peculiar echo of Virginia Woolf's final novel *Between the Acts*? Or was the enigma manifest there, what could not be assimilated by a particular form of professional spectating, in fact the dissolution of enigma? And might it be that what remains after that dissolution is neither some bare and unequivocal substructure of an ideological real, nor the impregnation of an underlying layer of the everyday with the power of the enigmatic, but something more obvious. What I want to suggest was being entertained that afternoon is the prescription that the familiar, the ordinary, the obvious, are all there is. This "lay theatre" seems to have absorbed, reproduced and systematically repudiated the various types of rationale put forward for theatrical practice, be that the unveiling power of critique, the festivity of collective self-representation, the undoing of the theatrical machinery, the production of ethical enigma, or "simple" pleasure and entertainment. This is precisely not to make a special claim for the aesthetic intelligence of this particular performance, which, as it "says" itself, is all these things and none of them. Instead, it is to remark the way in which its theatrical self-understanding, constituting what we might call (after Marx and others) a general intellect – a kind of unselfconscious common knowledge and capacity, has reached a particular degree of saturation. This is a type of knowledge that is truly "common sense". Today, the general intellect stages a certain type of openness to the world and to an ethos beyond the constraints of the present (typically figured as the neoliberal form of capitalism and representative democracies in critical discourse). As in *The Three Little Chavs*, stereotypes are refuted, stories acquire new endings and formal (theatrical) conventions can be ignored and inverted, capital is temporarily defeated, "we" are all having a good time, living the good life on holiday in England. But at the same time, it also knowingly enacts a kind of normative preservation order in which that alternative is disdained as a liberal myth of "radical" progress, always in plain sight but perpetually receding towards the horizon. One set of stereotypes is replaced by another, a story is just a story, inverted conventions do not usurp conventionality, let there be no illusions about what it means to have our place in the sun. In trying to account for the particular sense of spectatorial disarray occasioned by this performance, it is the shuttling between the two poles of this contradiction (neither paradox nor enigma) that seems significant, an oscillation "between something familiar that becomes agitated and something agitated that becomes familiar" (Virno 2008: 52).

To conclude prematurely: this condition militates against the ontological identification of an extra-ordinary, ethically charged "superpower" of dissensus or rupture that has been privileged in cultural theory and critique for a considerable period. As Hallward characterizes it, this power takes the form of "either indetermination (the interstitial, the hybrid, the ambivalent, the simulated, the undecidable, the chaotic . . .) or hyper-determination ('infinite' ethical obligation, divine transcendence, unconscious drive, traumatic repression, machinic automation . . .)" (Hallward, 2009: 16). Such forms find expression in the aesthetic or political event as a process of a truth, the public conceived as multitude, the infinite obligation to the Levinasian "other", the insurgency of the Lacanian "Real". These are only a few of the figures of supervenient immanence that have been articulated in the hope of providing an opening to a future from the permanent present of "business as usual". In light of the obvious and familiar crises (ecological, financial, imperial) of repetition that mark the contemporary, this opening seems to be less a response to the Leninist question of "what is to be done?", and more a question of "how"? In seeking a response to the question of "how?", the temptation is to replace the crisis of spectatorship – the privileged gap between knowledge, potential and act – with a prescriptive politics of action and participation. But if that substitution is not simply to replace one pole of the paradox of the spectator with its "ethical", activist other, than "how to spectate?" still ought to be a contradictory question that usefully troubles us.

Notes

1 For those not familiar with that term, 'chav' is derogatory slang for a stereotype of an uneducated, socially disruptive British underclass, identified by a fixation with fashions derived from American hip hop such as imitation gold, poorly made jewellery and fake designer clothing, combined with elements of British street fashion. It appears to have entered common usage in the UK during the late 1990s.

2 Neither is the solution to exchange this primacy of the expert observer with that of, for example, the expert practitioner, which maintains the binary of separation through a simple reversal of perspective – welcome though that might be in terms of redressing the balance.

References

Agamben, G. 1999. *The Man Without Content.* Translated by Georgia Albert. Stanford. Stanford University Press.

Gillespie, S. 2006. 'Giving Form to Its Own Existence: Anxiety and the Subject of Truth', *Cosmos and History: The Journal of Natural and Social Philosophy* [online], 2(2): 161–185, available at: http://www.cosmosandhistory.org/index.php/journal/article/view/33/66 – accessed 10 March 2010.

Hallward, P. 2006. 'Staging Equality', *New Left Review* 37: 109–129.

Hallward, P. 2009. 'The will of the people: notes towards a dialectical voluntarism,' *Radical Philosophy* 155 (May/June): 17–29.

Kelleher, J. 2008. 'How to Act, How to Spectate (Laughing Matter)', *Performance*

Research 13(4): 56–63.
Kelleher, J. 2009. *Theatre & Politics.* Basingstoke. Palgrave Macmillan.
Kershaw, B. 2007. 'Pathologies of Hope', *Performance Paradigm* [online], available at: http://www.performanceparadigm.net/journal/issue-3/interviews/pathologies-of-hope/ – accessed 10 March 2010.
Rancière, J. 2009. *Dissensus: On Politics and Aesthetics.* Translated by Steven Corcoran. London. Continuum.
Read, A. 2008. *Theatre, Intimacy and Engagement: The Last Human Venue*, Basingstoke. Palgrave Macmillan.
Ridout, N. 2009. *Theatre & Ethics.* Basingstoke. Palgrave Macmillan.
Virno, P. 2008. *Multitude: Between Innovation and Negation.* Translated by Isabella Bertoletti and James Cascaito. Cambridge, MA. MIT Press.

Crisis: Plates 1 and 2. *The Three Little Chavs,* 2006.

Crisis: Plates 3 and 4. *The Three Little Chavs,* 2006.

Crisis: Plates 5 and 6. *The Three Little Chavs,* 2006.

Troublesome Amateurs: Plate 7. *Übung,* Victoria Theatre, 2002.

Troublesome Amateurs: Plate 8. *Übung,* Victoria Theatre, 2002.

Troublesome Amateurs: Plate 9. *Übung,* Victoria Theatre, 2002.

Troublesome Amateurs: Plate 10. *Übung,* Victoria Theatre, 2002.

Troublesome Amateurs: Plate 11. *Kontakthof,* dir. Pina Bausch, Tanztheater Wuppertal, 2002. Photo © Ursula Kaufmann.

Troublesome Amateurs: Plate 12. *Kontakthof,* dir. Pina Bausch, Tanztheater Wuppertal, 2002. Photo © Ursula Kaufmann.

Troublesome Amateurs: Plate 13. *Kontakthof,* dir. Pina Bausch, Tanztheater Wuppertal, 2002. Photo © Ursula Kaufmann.

Troublesome Amateurs: Plate 14. *Kontakthof,* dir. Pina Bausch, Tanztheater Wuppertal, 2002. Photo © Ursula Kaufmann.

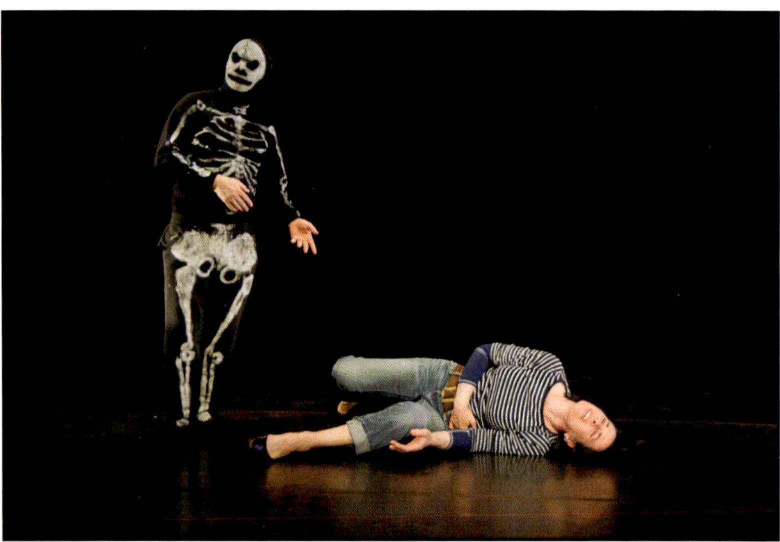

Corpsing: Plate 15. *Spectacular.* Forced Entertainment. Riverside Studios, London, 2008. Photo © Hugo Glendinning.

6

TROUBLESOME AMATEURS: THEATRE, ETHICS AND THE LABOUR OF MIMESIS

Adrian Kear

> The human is indissolubly linked with imitation: a human being only becomes human at all by imitating other human beings. In such behaviour, the primal form of love, the priests of authenticity scent traces of the utopia which could shake the structure of domination (Adorno 1974: 154).

> Because in effect mimesis is at play here. And because in mimesis, in effect, there is something troublesome. (Lacoue-Labarthe 1998: 63)

It should perhaps come as no surprise to lovers of the theatre that the foremost amongst Adorno's "priests of authenticity", Søren Kierkegaard, should turn to an image of performance to explain his philosophical conception of mimetic redemption. In *Works of Love*, he constructs a putative task for a dancer to "dance solo the dance he customarily dances with another" so that the spectator might observe the virtuosity of the movement, gesture and generation of emotion more readily than "if he were dancing with another actual person" (1998: 347). The etude's illustrative function is both to figure love's non-reciprocation and, more importantly for the direction of his argument, its "necessary" tendency to narcissistic self-absorption. The solitary dancer provides a motif that incarnates the lover's recollection – and mimetic resurrection – of a fundamentally *absent* other, whose role (being either dead or annihilated) is to draw attention to the self-communion of the one left performing.[1] The image thereby encapsulates the abstraction and reification that for Adorno characterizes Kierkegaard's obsession with the transcendental purity of a love driven solely by desire for redemption. Collapsing the subject–object relation replaces the logic of recognition with the rhetoric of seduction, and subsumes the historical materiality of the face-to-face situation into the indeterminate fantasy of "timeless" eternality. Thus the "radical inwardness" espoused by Kierkegaard and represented in the image of the dancer is eschewed by Adorno on the grounds of its failure "to comprehend subjectivity as a historical category", and the correlative suspension of the ethical that the work of love aspires to is likewise resisted as a dialectical and inter-subjective absurdity (2002: x–xii).

Adorno describes the parallel drawn between remembering the dead and the dancer dancing alone as being "both the worst and the best part" of Kierkegaard's analysis. At the same time as it demonstrates the limitations of love's aesthetic labours, it reveals in them the value of a non-reciprocal exchange "absolutely void of any barter, of any 'requital', and, therefore, the only unmutilated love permitted by our society" (Adorno 1939: 427; quoted in McDonald 2003: 88). In this respect, it is suggestive of a certain mimetic resistance to the logic of commodity capitalism, a disruption of its ability to mediate the purely economic terms of the relation. The work of love, like the work of art, is produced therefore through the capacity to generate "pure immediacy of feeling", and with it a longing for the "voluntarily involuntary" that offers a dispensation from the hard work of material production (Adorno 1974: 172, 222). Or at least it seems so. For the image of the dancer performing the solo *pas-de-deux* is given not as evidence of amateur passion but rather as an example of the mastery of technique; it *represents* the lover's emotional self-entanglement without itself becoming subject to it. The mimesis at work within the image both collapses the distance between self and other and at the same time maintains it, giving this portrayal of interiority a distinctively outward-looking dimension. As such it is indelibly theatrical, presented to an audience of onlookers whose very presence interrupts the solipsistic fiction of autoerotic inwardness.

So what if as theatre-lovers we were to start from this position instead, recognizing the primacy of inter-subjectivity and the persuasive power of the performance of authenticity? Perhaps concrete analysis of the theatre as a space of representation could produce some further critical insight into the relational forms taken by love's choreography of desire and identification? For "in the beginning is mimesis", says Mikkel Borch-Jacobsen (1988: 47), and it is the theatrical event par excellence that illustrates its operation. This can be seen in the literal meaning of representation as *Vorstellung*: posing *before* an audience, both in front of and prior to the assembly of actual spectators. In this way representation appears as an index of subjectivity, with visibility functioning as the very sign of subjective agency. As Kierkegaard's figure of the dancer goes some way to explain, *Vorstellung* as a work of love is at some level always self-reflective and self-constituting (though not necessarily self-conscious). Add to this Martin Heidegger's reworking of the Cartesian *cogitatio* and a clear picture emerges of the fundamental importance of representation as a modality of consciousness: "every 'I represent [I pose before myself] something' simultaneously represents a 'myself' [poses me before myself], me, the one representing (for myself, in my representing). Every human representing is – in a manner of speaking, and one that is easily misunderstood – a 'self'-representing [a 'self'-posing before oneself]" (1991: 106, quoted in Borch-Jacobsen 1991: 54). But, as Mikkel Borch-Jacobsen underlines, the positions of actor and onlookers are, strictly speaking, incompatible: the subject can either be one or the other. There is no space here for the professional performer's awareness of themselves performing – no Brechtian "not, but" to produce consciousness of mimetic doubling – just the simple "objectivity of the *Vorstellung*" in which "the lack of distinction between self and other – the mimesis – has to be acted out". And yet any intentional attempt to do so proves self-defeating, for "no sooner is it represented to the subject in the specular mode than it is betrayed" (Borch-Jacobsen 1988: 40). But in the theatrical situation proper – rather than its topographical mimesis in the imaging of consciousness – it is indeed such an intentional mode of representation that reveals as well as restrains the mechanism of identification. And the introduction of an audience further complicates matters considerably, for it creates confrontation with the reality of others – spectators no less, who are fully aware that what is presented before them is actively meant to be seen. The audience in effect bears witness to the fact of representation – to the subject's staging of itself as other in the mode of mimetic "acting" – and thereby to the coalescence of self and other made apparent through the theatrical exegesis. The spectatorial relation thus both mirrors and maintains representation in the mode of "posing before" which grounds identification, even though it threatens, at the same time, its "authentic" transparency and performative cohesion.

The fascinating indeterminacy of this relation – existing, perhaps, like Kierkegaard's dancer, somewhere between memory, fantasy, and premonition – is itself subjected to theatrical interrogation in the Victoria Theatre's *Übung* (2002). This production, whose title translates as "exercise" or "practice", provides a clear elaboration of what Borch-Jacobsen calls "corporeal-affective mimesis" (1991: 70). The company who perform it – who represent "themselves" in their alienation – are a group of six children only just beginning to enter their teens. Although amateurs by definition, their work is situated within a tightly orchestrated mise-en-scène produced by the director, Josse de Pauw, which effectively governs their movement, speech and timing. The performers' execution and technique is remarkable nonetheless, especially as the production depends upon them to achieve its effects. The stage environment they occupy comprises a large video screen and a playing space in front of it, bordered on either side by a row of chairs and a portable rail for hanging clothes. This ontologically "theatrical" scene is inhabited by the young people as the site of their socialization, brought into being by a peculiarly literal form of mimetic identification. Their "acting" in it consists of carefully executed imitations of the behaviour and language of the adults that appear in the film projected onto the screen in front of/behind them, with each performer "copying" exactly the movements of their specified models.

As each child performer mimes the actions of an adult actor, and vocalises the words of the text for them, the audience watches something like the performative construction of their "character" *in absentia*, with the film and the stage being cast into a temporal as well as spatial relation. A double mimesis is here being effectuated, with the live performers mirroring their filmic seniors in a display that demonstrates more than simply the problem of generation. On the one hand the children appear to be witnesses to the narrative of mimetic rivalry and marital infidelity that the film as a representation of bourgeois life seems to incorporate them into at the same time as it excludes them (as if they were secretly eavesdropping on their parents' conversation or peeking down the stairs at some dinner-party hi-jinx); on the other hand, they seem in their very presence to embody the very absence of children from the adults' lives, as if they represent their melancholia for the offspring they never had as much as the infant lost inside. The stage might in this sense function as the space of the film's memory and longing – although they exist in fact simultaneously – or, conversely, as the moment of its historical prefiguring. The children are in this sense witnessing what they themselves will become, their adult roles and relationships prescribed as the determinate effects of mimetic identification. And yet at the same time there is clearly some sort of bond of love between them, with the one figuring the other's absence in the solitude of their choreography.

This is perhaps best illustrated in a moving image that comes at the end of the show. In the film narrative, it is the morning after the night before, and the group of friends – reconciled once more after their outburst of drunken violence and infidelity – prepare for a walk in the woods. The children likewise dress up in outdoor clothes, exact copies of what their adult "models" are wearing. Although they fit perfectly, the incongruousness of the grown-up styling is plain to see. As if to accentuate the point, they assemble into a line for the curtain-call and hold their poses, looking out to the front, for a minute or two whilst the film actors meander uphill towards the camera. The effect of this pause in the action is deeply affecting, with time rushing back into the theatrical image even as it runs away on the screen. The young people's immobility as they face the future that has already taken place behind them, so to speak, is in this way almost liberating: they seem to hold onto the straitjacket of these identifications in order only to let go of them in an act of love as forgetting. The curtain call proper follows shortly, and what the performance seems to have borne witness to in its passing is something like the representation of the "ecstasy of alienation" (Borch-Jacobsen 1991: 70). By making visible the identificatory ruse of seeing oneself in the other, the production appears to hold out the promise of a transformation of mimesis through performance, in which the ties of history are opened up by the imaginative temporality of memory and fantasy to create a space of *alternative* possibility.

The imposing *mise-en-scène* of *Übung*, then, with its huge screen backdrop projecting adult figures in extreme close-up and "live" child actors modelling themselves against shadows cast upon it, brings back into focus the injunction against mimetic performance established by Plato in the *Republic*, Book X. As every first-year undergraduate knows, Plato disbars the young guardians of the "ideal" society from participating in any form of mimetic activity on the grounds of its transformative potentiality. The principal reason for so doing is to inoculate against the destabilizing effects of mimesis as a mode of "yielding" to alterity,[2] which might corrupt by either directly performing acts of "self-likening" such as acting in plays or reciting poetry, or by vicarious exposure to their communicative effects through the "sympathetic" witnessing of "other people's suffering" in the audience experience (605c–606b). This latter concern extends considerably Plato's otherwise restricted use of mimesis within the *Republic*'s conceptual economy to describe a type of speech made "under the name of another" (III.392c–398b). It is almost as if his struggle to stress the dangers of imitation in affecting the integrity of "body, voice and mind" (III.395d1–3) results in an unconscious redoubling of its ascribed affective potency, "since, when one has nurtured and strengthened one's capacity for pity on the lives of others, it is difficult to suppress it in one's own sufferings" (X.606b7–8). The genie of mimesis is thereby let out of its subjective container, constituting itself as a general threat to the construction and maintenance of stable "character" (*êthos*). Mimesis and ethics as such are therefore placed in direct opposition to each another – a manoeuvre repeated by the Kierkegaardian dancer – albeit through a forced separation that Plato, as a self-confessed lover of performance, can only imagine reluctantly (X.607e). However, elsewhere in the *Republic* the injunction against mimesis appears to be applied only to the former mode of "impersonation"; Book III even suggests that the "recognition" of both good and evil characters in dramatic representation might play a productive role in the development of ethical "understanding" and detached critical judgement (III.396a4–6). As Stephen Halliwell has demonstrated, the rejoining of ethics and mimesis might not be impossible for Plato to envisage. He argues that the initially restricted perspective on mimesis, which is found more frequently in Plato's writings, is suggestive of a repressed counter-argument permitting the staging of theatre "in the well-regulated city but for barring citizens from performing in it and for leaving this task to slaves and aliens" (Halliwell 2002: 79–80). In other words, the problem with mimesis emerges as a problem, in effect, of *amateur* participation: as long as lovers of the theatre refrain from the temptations of actual board-treading, professional actors and mimics might reasonably be allowed to continue to produce the goods – if not "the good" – within it.

Of course, such a division of labour has no place within the "proper" constitution of the ideal society. Indeed, the very problem of mimesis, as Plato sees it, is its introduction of certain divisiveness into the mobilization of subjective potentialities, producing in the process a multiplication of alternate possibilities. It is not without coincidence that, as Philippe Lacoue-Labarthe has observed, the first discussion of mimesis in the *Republic* occurs at the outset of the debate about the proper education of the guardians, suggesting that it is not "principally a problematic of the lie" which concerns mimesis, "but instead a problematic of the *subject* . . . of the subject in its relation to language" (1998: 125). Speaking "under the name of another" is troublesome to Plato in that it offers a change of perspective at the expense of moral certitude, proliferating subjective possibilities – ways of being otherwise – in a manner that exceeds the limitations imposed by his unitary conception of *êthos*. Nonetheless, this structural constraint on mimesis as a creative activity does not prevent him from seeing, as has been stated, the value of mimetic products as ethical guides for human behaviour and useful representations of good "character" (III.401a–d). In short, Plato appears to distinguish between mimesis as a labour of production and as a mode of consumption – terms inimical, perhaps, to his delineation of the integrity of the ideal society but revealing, all the more, of mimesis's foundational centrality. As Lacoue-Labarthe summarily puts it, "mimesis has always been an economic problem; it is the problem of economy" (1998: 124). So when, for example, Plato's attention turns from the austerity of his ideal state to its "real" counterpoint in Athens, the "city of luxury", mimesis becomes implicated in the proliferation of the very forms of the market economy – in the expansion of goods and services and the insidious multiplication of disreputable professions (III.373). Mimesis is thereby configured as economy's effective *modus operandi*, responsible for "generalised depropriation . . . uncontrollable polyvalence . . . the exacerbation of desire . . . In fact, almost 'Capital'" (Lacoue-Labarthe 1998: 124). And this is perhaps the crux of the Platonic extension of the injunction against impersonation: mimesis soon supplants "mere" imitation with a much more destabilizing mode of social production. Lacoue-Labarthe identifies this mechanism as "demiurgy": the work of making something on behalf of the *demos*, of "installing" it within the community; "establishing" it, so to speak. For him, "only the demiurgic interpretation of mimesis" – precisely the expansive one offered by Plato in the *Republic* Book X – "permits the disengaging of its essence" as the labour of making, the "disinstallation" of its technical effect. Its determinate negativity cannot therefore be discounted too readily. The emphasis placed by Plato on the question of "fabrication" serves to confirm, in fact, that "the essence of mimesis is not imitation, but production" (Lacoue-Labarthe 1998: 80) and that the trouble he has with it is with the very work put into the "work of art" as such.

In other words – and mimesis always uses "other words" – what is troublesome in mimesis is not just its slipperiness as a concept (which appears to occupy at least three positions simultaneously: as "imitation" [qua representation]; as "creation" [qua production]; and as sensate "reception" [qua interpretation]),[3] but its transmutation of ethics from the domain of known qualities to a sphere of pure potentiality. Mimesis thereby puts the ethical into suspension – making it possibility rather than actuality – by inhering it with the capacity not to "be" (Agamben 1998: 45–46). Here it acquires a temporal orientation towards future possibilities as well as past opportunities, making it an imaginative vehicle of infinite capacity and limitless productivity. The agency governing this operation is the technç of artistic creativity, generating as well as representing ethical choices between contrasting experiences of lived reality that interrupts the continuum of linear history. At the same time as mimesis addresses itself to an encounter with exteriority – to the very "otherness" manifest in the fact of materiality – it also articulates the immanent possibility of things being configured or "occasioned" differently. This is the term Heidegger utilizes in 'The Question Concerning Technology' to account for the possible ways that "what is not yet present" can "arrive into presencing" (1977: 317); or, to put it slightly differently, how potentiality might be realized in actuality (Agamben 1999: 183).[4] It is derived in turn from Plato's *Symposium*, in which the ethic of mimesis is given a distinctively temporal inflection as that which "presences" transient appearance: "Every occasion for whatever passes beyond the non-present and goes forward into presencing is *poiēsis,* bringing-forth" (205b, trans. in Heidegger 1977: 317). Heidegger argues that *poiēsis* is a naturally-guided process through which immanence is brought into being as an "irruption" of presence (such as "the bursting of a blossom into bloom"); its "manufactured" form in the arts and crafts is an extension of this principle whereby "the irruption belonging to bringing-forth" is manifested "not in itself, but in *another*" (1977: 317, emphasis added). Mimesis might be said, then, to twist the perspective more than slightly, to be the agent of the "irruption" of something like alterity. Heidegger seeks to contain this possibility by insisting that the "bringing-forth" effected by *poiēsis* is advanced only in relation to an ordered – and ordained – "destining" (1977: 330). It is with this teleology in mind that he asserts that the end of *technē* consists in the "revelation" of an essential truth [*alētheia*] rather than in its production from scratch; "bringing-forth" is thus a matter of presentation [*Darstellung*] rather than representation [*Vorstellung*] as such. The labour involved in making art the occasion through which this "revelation" happens is characterized by Heidegger as "neither only a human activity nor a mere means within such an activity" (1977: 326). It is rather the work of the work of art itself to bring its own truthfulness about. But the gap between the technical and the ethical is at least part of the problem the dynamic of mimesis poses for Plato in *Republic* X; accomplishment, after all, is not equivalent to achievement (602d) and "verisimilitude, the look of the real, should not be confused with veracity" or *alētheia* itself (Halliwell 2002: 59). The space mimesis opens is, in effect, a temporal fissure in re-presentation, which may equally be occupied by a tendentious intentionality as by a divinely inspired "saving power" (Heidegger 1977: 337), creating thereby the opportunity for a purposive shaping of the world in the likeness of humanity.[5] And this, for Plato, is at least in part constitutive of its disruptive capacity as well as its ethical potentiality. Mimesis doesn't merely facilitate the formalization and arrival of appearance, nor does it simply enable the otherwise latent content of the image to "speak"; it provides a framework for the active labour of making sense of the world through the exercise of ethical judgement and the establishment of moral value (Halliwell 2002: 131–132). As such, it places the tools of poiēsis firmly within human hands, making "man" responsible for the fashioning of its various possibilities, and limitations.

For Aristotle, as for Heidegger following him, mimetic practice displays an intentionality that is predicated upon an essentially "natural" origin, and as such can be ordered relatively harmoniously. In the *Physics* he offers the famous formulation: *he technē mimeitai ten phusin* ("art imitates nature", 194a), along with the more helpful extrapolation that art not only imitates the natural world but simulates nature's creativity by "perfecting" or completing what nature itself is unable to bring to fruition (199a). This is important because it illustrates that he conceives of mimesis, even more clearly than Plato, as a guide to *eudaimonia*, or human happiness. Mimesis for Aristotle moves beyond its "restricted" form as imitation to become the "general" principle which, as Lacoue-Labarthe explains, "reproduces nothing given (which thus re-produces nothing at all), but which *supplements* a certain deficiency in nature, its incapacity to do everything, to organise everything, to make everything its work – *produce* everything" (1998: 255). This "productive mimesis" imitates nature as a creative energy; "it accomplishes, carries out, *finishes* natural production as such" (Lacoue-Labarthe 1998: 256). In short, mimesis is thus figured by Aristotle as a productive principle governed by *poiēsis* as the process of "making". The *Poetics* further codifies and regulates its general positivity by seeking to ensure its "intentional grounding" in the institutions and conventions of tragic form (Halliwell 2002: 156). This entails the subordination of "character" (*êthos*) to "plot" (*muthos*), and the stipulation that it is "action" (*praxis*) that mimesis "imitates" rather than "men" [sic]. Whilst on the one hand this normalizes and renders rationally coherent the art of tragedy (Diamond 1997: x), it also has the effect of shifting the emphasis from mimesis as "substitution" (impersonation, imitation) to its role as "supplementation" (production, creation) – to the realization of a certain *theatrical* ethic that lies less in the recognition of ethical universals than in the fact that poetic mimesis, in essence, "always produces a theatre, a representation. That is to say, *another representation* – or the presentation of *something other*, which was not yet there, given, or present" (Lacoue-Labarthe 1998: 257). The theatre, in this way, "exemplifies general mimesis" by providing a means of imagining the world *otherwise*; as Plato knew, "theatrical mimesis, in other words, provides the model for general mimesis" (Lacoue-Labarthe 1998: 257), and its principal ethical problematic lies in the bringing to appearance, or imaging, of what is not yet (or no longer) present.

The temporal direction of mimesis is therefore irremediably split: oriented towards the future, it produces in the present an image of what is to come that is always-already conjured from the past. Theatrical performance takes place within this temporal torsion, "seizing in the instant" the time of the future as that which discloses the forgotten memory of repressed history (Düttmann 2002: 22–23). Its mimesis thereby figures the inability of representation to proceed without interruption, the intervention of that unpredictable agent of communication that enables the past to be reimagined "from the perspective of redemption" (Düttmann 2000: 44). As Walter Benjamin argues, the interruptive "flash" of mimetic recognition suspends the moment of the image's historical origination, orienting it instead towards the future possibility of its temporal transformation (1978: 335–336). History thus appears as the condition of futurity, and futurity the framework for the recognition of historical materiality, whilst mimesis takes on an atemporal characteristic, referring back to an ahistorical time before time, or, more specifically, a time before *economy*. For Benjamin, the transient appearance of the mimetic image acts upon the perceiver as a reminder of a mode of existence anterior to capitalism and its attendant reification of social relations, temporalizing in effect their hegemonic institutionalization. It therefore offers a glimpse of an alternative order of things by looking backwards and forwards simultaneously, showing both how the current state of affairs operates and how its destructive effects might be repaired. Mimesis is here once more bound up with human praxis, providing both a way of knowing the world in its constructedness and a means of recognizing the capacity for human beings to transform it into something different.

This is implicit also in Adorno's deployment of the concept to account for the progress of "civilization" through its systematic appropriation and repression. For Adorno, mimesis has the status of a foundational ur-category of human activity, equating to a mode of existence that pre-exists social subjugation to the highly codified and regulated network of power relations that combine to produce what he calls the condition of "heteronomy" (1991: 168). It functions in effect as a "magical term" within his complex theoretical framework – invoked, but never defined directly, as the oblique name given to the elusive and enigmatic exercise of freedom within human relations (Jameson 1990: 64). Mimesis is thus figured as a destabilizing element resisting generalized conformity to heteronomy, and acting, further, as a constant reminder of the possibility of alterity. As such, its performativity is necessarily circumscribed and attenuated to the service of reproductive economy; such a manoeuvre, he argues, "has been the condition for civilization" for centuries. "Uncontrolled mimesis is outlawed" within this situation, because "civilization has replaced the organic adaptation to others and mimetic behaviour proper, by organised control of mimesis, in the magical phase; and finally by work, in the historical phase" (Adorno and Horkheimer 1979: 181). For Adorno, then, mimesis is subject to controlled mimesis under the sign of Capital (for which read civilization, or, for that matter, totalitarianism), which converts this "mimesis of mimesis" into a productive principle of bourgeois society and thereby attempts to banish mimesis proper entirely (1979: 185).

Such a totalizing process is, however, inevitably subject to disruption. For Adorno, it is the work of art that offers the vehicle for mimesis's reanimation, providing a terrifying glimpse of archaic prehistory and with it the promise of future possibility. "Artworks have the immanent character of being an act", he writes, "and this endows them with the quality of being momentary and sudden." As such they provide a jolt to consciousness – an interruption – whose intervention facilitates the surprise "appearance of an other". The experience of looking at them is, therefore, one of affective temporalization, for "under patient contemplation works begin to move. To this extent they are truly after-images of the primordial shudder in the age of reification" (Adorno, 1997: 79). The troubling aspect of this encounter is more than the uncanny recognition of a ghostly "apparition" – it amounts to the appearance of an *image* that ruptures the social relation. Faced with sudden and unforeseen exposure to "the appearance of the nonexistent as if it existed", the subject subjectively experiences the otherness of the past and the alterability of the future (Adorno, 1997: 82). The aesthetic "irruption" thus effects a temporary interruption – "an intermezzo of freedom" (Adorno 1974: 175) – during which the existing order of things might come to be seen differently. This could be called the space of *imagination*, through which the subject translates the inscrutability of the primordial image into the language of historical possibility. For Adorno, this is also a point of *identification*, an opening out towards the other in the form of a "mimesis reflex" that seeks to re-establish the integrity of the subject through a process of "self-conservation, self-constitution, and self-affirmation" forged in the image of a self-authenticating "nature" (Düttmann, 2000: 86–87). In other words, the other that makes its appearance through the mimetic work of art is the other of nature as pure potentiality, released from the ties of its instrumentalization in the social. And the viewer identifies with this as a peculiarly human particularity – capable and incapable simultaneously – and apprehending in the instant the possible overcoming of institutionalized mimicry through the promise of mimetically engendered alterity.

But this optimism can only really be sustained momentarily. The return of mimesis in the work of art is also a return to its rational codification in a highly organized signifying system, for "the ratio which supplants mimesis is not simply its counterpart. It is itself mimesis: mimesis unto death" (Adorno and Horkheimer, 1979: 57). This then is the hyper-mimetic world of exchange rationality, in which everything can be substituted for anything regardless of purpose or similarity. In its inexorable economy, the work of art appears as "pure use value" – as a thing in itself – in order to sustain the "abstract character of exchange value" against which it may be judged as a unique singularity (Adorno, 1982: 279). As such, it occupies the position of a fetish – revealing at the same time as concealing its inverse affirmation of commodity relations in consumer society. The more "priceless" a work of art is, the higher its price becomes, and its presumed purposelessness serves a practical purpose in maintaining the values of the ever-expanding market. It is also in this sense that "avant-garde" artworks can afford to adopt the pose of a thoroughgoing opposition to bourgeois society, as art's antisocial status – derived from its claim to autonomy – is in fact the product of the dialectical unity of identity and non-identity (Jameson, 1990: 177). As Adorno succinctly puts it, art "becomes social by virtue of its oppositional position to society itself, a position it can only occupy by defining itself as autonomous" (1984: 321). And yet, of course, art is always-already thoroughly "social", being itself the historical product of social relations of production and social forces of production which "return in the very form of the work, divested of their facticity, because artistic labour is also social labour; works of art are also the products of social labour" (Adorno, 1984: 355). The work in the work of art is therefore the index of its imbrication in existing relations of production, of its inescapable attachment to the world of commodity fetishism. In this respect there is nothing "unique" about it, for the productive forces at work in the work of art are not exclusive to it, but are derived, at least in some sense, from the totality of those at play within its wider socio-economic context. For Adorno, there is nothing that can be "performed or invented within the work of art that does not have its equivalent – in however latent a form – within social production itself" (Adorno, 1984: 355). But this is not to say that its practice of making can be reduced to an ideological formula or process of reproduction; after all, the mimetic gesture of the "authentic" work of art in the age of capitalism is directed towards the deliberate eschewal of "the mere imitation of that which already is" (Adorno and Horkheimer, 1979: 18). Artistic mimesis is, therefore, to be understood as much as an activity of unmaking the "mimesis of mimesis" as a process of remaking it into a new historical form.

To this extent the labour of making the work of art can be seen to sustain itself in the belief that it is only through the process of self-evident fabrication that it remains possible to speak truthfully. As Adorno explains, "in the face of the lie of the commodity world, even the lie that denounces it becomes corrective" (1974: 44). Under capitalism's relations of production, however, this quickly becomes co-opted as just another form of professional activity. The artist's technical competence and aura of expertise soon segue with the inescapable problem of earning a living, producing a producer with unrivalled skills and highly marketable labour power. The structural function of the artist as the maker of works of critical distinction is thereby rendered subservient to their role within the general economy of commodity exchange and the harnessing of social forces of production. In other words, under capitalism the artist is no less alienated from the products of their labour than the rest of us, for the very process of their making in the prevailing social conditions inevitably transforms them into something else. Which perhaps begs an interesting question: If the professional functions as the sign of art's irremediable translation into the language of the commodity, perhaps the space of its trans-valuation could be found within what might remain as the space of amateurism? After all, is it not "the bourgeois idea of love", as "a dispensation from work", that alone "transcends" the categories of "bourgeois society" (Adorno, 1974: 172)? Adorno would no doubt be sceptical, dismissive even, of such a suggestion, reminding us of capitalism's control over leisure as well as work through its relations of production. For if labour power is a commodity in capitalist society – in which labour itself is necessarily reified – then the "free time" that it purchases is equally commodified. Adorno argues convincingly that capitalism reifies "free time" as an illusory freedom from work and shibboleth of subjective well-being, whose very existence is in reality the product of "the totality of social conditions, which continues to hold people under its spell". The unity of labour and leisure is in this sense complete, so that "even where the hold of the spell is relaxed, and people are at least subjectively convinced that they are acting of their own free will, this will is itself shaped by the very same forces which they are seeking to escape in their hours without work" (1991: 162). According to Adorno, then, "free time is nothing more than a shadowy continuation of labour" in which the subject unconsciously extends the "conditions of heteronomy" to the point at which they "become heteronomous for themselves" (1991: 168). In these circumstances it would appear that the capacity for agency – and agentful creativity – all but evaporates entirely, leaving a totalizing system in total control of human destiny. But Adorno also concedes that this is something of a false impression, with even capitalist society being unable to achieve such an absolute ambition entirely. To do so, after all, would risk losing our productive potentiality, or at least diminishing the ability to appropriate it in the form of the commodity. Perhaps it is with this glimmer of opportunity, then, that we sense the chance possibility that "free time" might eventually be made into "freedom proper" (Adorno, 1991: 170).

This is not to say that the amateur as such should become the figure for the reanimation of art's liberating idealism. After all, the very notion of the amateur is itself the product of capitalism's rigorous demarcation of the division of labour that ensures, concomitantly, the predominance of "professionalism". It is not, equally, to say that the compulsion to utilize "free time" to undertake art-making activities might itself be something of a godsend in enabling the straitjacket of subservience to economy to be sidestepped effectively; as we have seen, to do so would be merely to uphold an illusory image of "unmediated life within a completely mediated total system" (Adorno, 1991: 164) which also leaves the imperative of wage labour effectively intact. Indeed, the amateur artist is left having to do something else to earn a living as well – such as bar-tending, data processing or, for that matter, academic writing – thereby confirming the fallacy of their work's existence outside the boundaries of exchange rationality. In the inexorable logic of capitalism, then, the amateur, however passionate and intense, has the "inferiority" of their work announced automatically; the simple fact of not having been paid for making it is enough to signify its redundancy or lack of merit. The absence of exchange value erodes any conception of its use value, and the labour of making is thereby consigned to the diminished category of a mere "hobby". This suggests that the work itself 'has something superfluous about it" – inevitably so given that "under prevailing conditions it would be erroneous and foolish to expect or demand that people should be genuinely productive in their free time; for productivity – the ability to bring forth something that was not already there – is the very thing that has been eradicated from them" (Adorno, 1991: 167). The amateur artist is thus, in this conception, nothing more than a cipher for art's attenuation to capitalism – imitating, in effect, the professional's mimesis of mimesis in its authentic operation. Here mimesis serves economy absolutely remorselessly, to the extent that they become totally integrated as a form of hybridized "economimesis".

And yet, its productive – and disruptive – capacity can never be eliminated completely. The mimesis of mimesis as creative activity might actually reveal something like the index of its appropriation under conditions of heteronomy. Whilst remaining disdainful of their imitative and derivative qualities, Adorno maintains that the amateur's "pseudo-activities are fictions and parodies of the same productivity which society on the one hand incessantly calls for, but on the other holds in check and, as far as the individual is concerned, does not really desire at all" (1991: 168). Although he doesn't afford them any credibility as such, it is not too difficult to see how the space of the amateur might be endowed with *critical* potentiality. By drawing attention to the gap between passion and achievement, enthusiasm and accomplishment, the amateur practitioner offers an alternative figure for artistic labour. Moreover, by simultaneously existing within and yet gesturing beyond the rigid boundaries of work and play imposed by capitalism, the figure of the amateur stands in for their temporalization. By both referring back to a moment preceding art's professionalization and opening out the future possibility of its decommodification, the mimesis of amateurism, in other words, provides an opportunity for thinking outside the limits of the existing relations and forces of production. Or, it at least appears to. And appearances, whilst often deceptive, can also, of course, prove corrective.

Certainly contemporary performance seems to have something of a fascination with the figure of the amateur and their embodiment of a non-reciprocal love of theatre. The writer and director Richard Foreman, for example, has consistently articulated a desire for the stage to adopt the "authenticity" of amateur performers over and above the studied perfectionism of professional actors. He describes the latter as atypical representatives of ordinary humanity, whose representational qualities are limited to the production of "strong emotions" and a rare "charisma" that in effect marks them out from the rest of the population. Of course, this could amount to nothing more than a critique of a limited technique and an excess of passion – like that mounted by Diderot against the nephew of Rameau – but Foreman instead identifies it as a generic failing and the core of his problem with so-called "acting". He insists that he is interested in "seeing people on stage", not actors, and therefore encourages his performers to display their idiosyncrasies and individuality in a manner not masked by actorly technique. He explains that, in his early experiments in theatre-making, "what interested me was taking people from real life, nonactors, and putting them on stage to allow their real personalities to have a defiant impact on the conventional audience". And so it appears that what is at stake here is a valorization of the capacity to "be yourself" over and above the ability to become "other" – a deprecation of acting as a quintessentially mimetic form of performance. The "real" person is invoked as an index of authenticity, whose authority is derived in turn from an "extreme naturalness" projected by the performer's inhabitation of their own body. This, Foreman claims, "had a disruptive effect on the audience, because what the spectator was watching was a particular kind of naturalness that had been banished from the theatre" through a peculiarly inverted form of theatrical snobbery. As he explains, "the theatre works very hard to keep out awkward, amateurish, wooden performances" from the purview of its scenes; so the fascination for him was "to bring that area of naturalness into the theatre, simply because it hadn't been seen" (Foreman, 1992: 32–33). But of course Foreman is not here speaking of the hopeless imitations of acting that take place evening after evening in the amateur theatre proper – the mimesis of mimesis's professionalization in which the performer simply "mimes the mimetician" (Lacoue-Labarthe, 1998: 263) – but rather a "new" form of amateurism brought under the expert control of the theatre director. Here task-based activity or simple blocking stands in for the development of "character" and narrative diegesis, with the effect that the performer emerges primarily as a function of the *mise-en-scène*. Foreman privileges the "nonactor" not so much for their lack of technique but rather for their ability to be manipulated by his "techniques", leaving the performer's body – and its resistances – in the service of the authorial construction of meaning. This use of performers is, then, more like the organized control of mimetic activity rather than its total suppression, in which "the real" is sutured to "the really made up" in order to establish the latter's efficacy (Taussig, 1993: 86). Here he appears to share the dream of a theatrical über-technique – initiated by Kleist and continued by Gordon Craig – that would overcome the limitations of the actor entirely. The director appears to acknowledge as much by reverting, subsequently, to the employment of professional actors in an effort to develop an alternative set of performance vocabularies requisite to the production of his avant-garde aesthetic (Foreman, 1992: 36). So, whilst "awkwardness" and the appearance of "amateurism" remain the hallmarks of the performer in a Foreman production, these theatrical reality-effects are themselves subject to the most intense forms of technical construction. It should not, therefore, be altogether surprising that it takes a true professional to master their intentional manipulation into spontaneous appearing.

What Foreman's work appears to inaugurate on this occasion is, therefore, a partial extension – though recuperation – of the actor's technique. The haphazard mistakes and impromptu failings that for centuries had been a nightmare waiting to happen are here intentionalized and remotivated as the site and source of the performer's peculiar "talent". This – once described by Rousseau in Platonic mode as "the art of disguising oneself, of assuming a character other than one's own, of appearing different from what one is, of becoming deliberately impassioned, of saying something other than what one thinks as naturally as if one actually thought it, and of finally forgetting one's own place by taking that of another" (1968: 163) – is then seemingly turned on its head. The performer's task appears instead to be one of self-presentation, accentuating the pure semblance of what one actually is, and in the process becoming other than someone simply "pretending" to be another. Put simply, "acting" is sublated into a generalized field of performer activity in order to secure the mimetic effect of authenticity. Hence the sure signs of failure in a conventional actor's technique – coughing, corpsing, unconscious twitching, recollective panic and those telltale lapses in concentration – are less the products of reality's interruption of an all-embracing fiction than the indexes of its deliberate conversion into theatrical codification. So what were originally repositories of the real life underpinning the stage illusion – whose "irruption" might otherwise produce "spontaneous disclosures of the human" (Bayly, 2002: 44) – are now once again subjected to mimetic appropriation.

This can be seen quite clearly, for example, in the recent work of Forced Entertainment, whose *Disco Relax* (1999) and *First Night* (2002) feature performers manipulating their mastery over the cardinal sins of acting in the forms of uncontrollable laughter and incapacitating stage fright respectively. By isolating and over-extending these moments of breakdown, incompetence and enforced recovery, the company partially rehabilitates acting through the creation a "new" performance vocabulary based on its wholesale deconstruction. This has become something of a sine qua non for postmodernist theatre-making: the overcoming, through mimesis, of the mimetic mode of theatrical representation. What it effectively draws attention to is the fact that the theatre, despite its best post-Brechtian attempts at honesty, can in the end only ever have recourse to the truth of its fakery; the dissimulation of acting is therefore merely the sign of the pretence of not pretending. This, of course, Forced Entertainment well know, as their accumulation of ever more ostentatiously theatrical props and costumes – from sequined suits and bewigged clown faces to the heads of pantomime horses – demonstrates. Their work seems to be seeking after the indivisible remainder of theatre's true illusion, to be glimpsed, perhaps, in the moment of its interruption by the surprise accident, disaster or fiasco, or made visible through the remorseless exposure of the performer's limitations and vulnerability. It is as if the theatre's capacity inadvertently to produce the human, all too human, is here intentionalized as the framework for their theatre-making. As the scenic arrangement draws the spectator's attention to its bespoke artificiality and playful mocked-upness – with no attempt being made to make anything look "real", just really "theatrical" – the performers are often moved in the opposite direction, appearing to reveal themselves in their hopelessness, nervousness and desperation. The face-to-face relation, literalized in the end-on scenic configuration, provides the opportunity for the audience to encounter them directly, seduced into an exchange of looks and feelings, the glare of the footlights notwithstanding. This, at least, is how *First Night* opens: the performers, one-by-one, shuffle across the forestage and confront the audience with a fixed cheesy grin – the enigmatic emblem of every actor's basic desire and demand: "love me". The gesture is as pathetic as it is comic, instantly producing ripples of laughter but also being held long enough to discomfort and disrupt the expectation of entertainment. As such, it also figures something like a moment of refusal – an unwillingness on the part of the company to accept the terms of the stage's requirement that they produce something gratifying. The performance – and the performers – are thereby held in suspension, halted, frozen, arrested right here at the beginning. The longer it goes on, the more it seems an impasse has been reached, with the inertia induced laughter slowly subsiding into sighs of boredom and frustration. Yet these hapless manic grimaces seem to articulate all too visibly the Beckettian dynamic of the actor's ethic – "I can't go on, I will go on" – and the show proceeds accordingly. Something similar happens with the extended duration of Cathy Naden's hysterical, drunken laughter in the middle of *Disco Relax*: a kind of theatrical longueur is created which takes dramatic time out of the theatrical equation, imploding narrative temporality and foregrounding the act of pure presentation. This deliberate interruption has the effect of suspending the performance's mimetic cohesion, drawing attention instead to the performer themselves and their embodiment of somatic resistance to its semiotic seriousness (Ridout, 2000). Naden's inability to stop laughing – intentional as it is – takes the audience only so far with her; after that, it becomes an exhibition of virtuoso incongruousness. What it reveals is the inherence of real time within the theatre's otherwise rigorous attempts to fabricate it, creating a kind of de-syncopated rhythm in which the actual and the imaginary coalesce only intermittently. The audience might experience this at the level of frustration or, just a likely, through an identificatory empathy with the pain and pathos of enforced hilarity. Perhaps what this indicates is, then, simply the isolation of the performer under conditions of alienation.

Something not dissimilar might be said to be happening when the amateur proper comes to occupy the stage, except on this occasion the laughter is likely to originate in the audience and gravitate in the performer's direction. There's an episode I recall from my formative years that seems to epitomize this nicely: I'm watching a village-hall production of *A Gang Show* or something, in which a middle-aged woman, in a blue-green sequined dress, has the onerous task of keeping time to the swaying motion of a song and dance routine. She fails miserably, being either always behind or ahead of the rhythm established by the rest of the company. And, unfortunately, the upshot of this de-syncopation is genuine risibility, with the audience – and me especially – unable to restrain ourselves from laughing at her directly. Such a "momentary anaesthesia of the heart" (Bergson, 1980: 64) is produced in the spectator through witnessing a gap open up between intention and achievement, a tear in the fabric of the performance that is usually sutured by the performer's technique. The laughter it induces is to this extent irrepressible acknowledgement of the fragile humanity exposed to view by this experience, a humiliating collapsing inward of the performer's attempts at mimetic externalization and extension. There is, I have been trying to suggest, something in this incompetence and awkwardness that is more than simply amusing, producing the comic and the pathetic as the identificatory effects of these moments of extreme vicariousness. It is this immanent yet elusive quality that contemporary performance seems to reify in its mimetic reproduction of such situations, parodying but also eulogizing their profound naïveté.

This is perhaps why the amateur performer seems increasingly to be professional theatre's newest form of "hot property". The display of amateur bodies, attempting something for which they are not trained or used, is no longer confined to the living hell of reality TV. Indeed, it was Pina

Bausch's *Kontakthof* (2002) that prompted my *Gang Show* memory. This masterful production, a revival of a work made some twenty-four years previously, was remarkable largely for being performed by a company of twenty-odd dance-hall amateurs all aged over the official retirement threshold of sixty-five. These senior citizens, drawn from the Wuppertal locality, and past the "sell-by date" of their productivity, had the onerous responsibility of dancing all the steps, performing all the gestures, and remembering all the routines in the original choreography, which was initially devised and staged by an ensemble at least a generation younger than themselves, two-and-a-half decades previously. But Bausch makes no concessions to their apparent lack of vigour or technical prowess, having drilled them – remorselessly, one suspects – into performing the material just as she expects. Indeed, it is precisely their flabbiness and self-consciousness that she utilizes as a reality-effect, allowing their age and genuine enthusiasm to endow the choreography with something like the "aura" of authenticity. The performance consists of over three hours of physically demanding, theatrically intense sequences, in which the performers reprise some of the now classic moments of the Tanztheater repertory. They move through ensemble configurations of tightly organized rhythm and duration, to playful moments of seemingly sporadic interrelation. In one image they advance towards the audience beating time with the steps of their feet; in another, they circle the stage in a hermetic display of their own exuberant enjoyment.

They exchange stories and intimacies, narrate "disturbing details of their past lives and loves", and demonstrate an ambiguous "tenderness and aggression" towards one another in scenes of calculated violence and seduction (Mackrell, 2002).

The performers pair-off to create the most unlikely couples, undertaking pas-des-deux with surprise actions such as discarding shoes and clothing, and rekindling adolescent sexuality through furtive glances and the occasional chance groping.

Accompanying all this is a mellifluous soundtrack of vaguely familiar tunes from the twenties and thirties, engrained with gramophone originality, which has the effect of inscribing the performance within the indeterminate space of theatrical memory. It's almost as if the stage itself – designed to be reminiscent of a village hall or ubiquitous social club venue – is endowed with mimetic significance, creating the illusion of a world in which the ageing performers themselves might be presumed to have once loved and lived. But interestingly enough, their words and memories are no more their own than the strange movements to which they have had to discipline their bodies, created as they were from the original cast's childhood recollections of their parents' social milieu and their own singular experiences of professional auditioning (Parry, 2002). What the amateur performers have been asked to do is, in effect, to give their bodies over to the reanimation of other people's materials and material fantasies. The mimesis involved in this is therefore double and split: the company are required to reproduce the devised choreography in order to endow it with a borrowed authenticity. The mimesis of mimesis is in this respect complete, with the performers themselves – for all their faltering hesitancy – perfecting the appearance of an *anthropomorphized* humanity.

The amateur dancers in *Kontakthof* to this extent function as something of a representational fetish, stretching the semblance of identity between actor and role past the point at which "the fetish character of the commodity lays claim to actual people" and expropriates the very stuff of their subjectivity (Adorno, 1991: 165). One scene in particular sticks in the memory for the way it trades upon this relation, exploiting quite deliberately the apparent bond between the materiality of the body and its representational function. It revolves around a moment of "competition" between the elderly performers, in which one by one they attempt to dance a solo, following the on-stage instructions to produce "big juicy circles" as they advance towards the audience gyrating their hips. The results are predictably awkward and embarrassing for both performers and audience, who become locked into watching this excruciating circuit of auto-presentation. They laugh heartily at the display of bodily inflexibility – not one of the OAPs is capable of achieving the objective – as if in acknowledgement of the absurdity of overvaluing physical "technique". And yet at the same time there is something profoundly disturbing about the exhibition of the gap between intention and realization being manifested at the level of the performer's body, a kind of inverse objectification that serves to confirm their alienation in the performance's theatrical economy. The audience's laughter is perhaps the index of the significance of this: is it addressed to the performers directly or offered self-reflexively, as comic recognition of a shared risibility (Critchley, 2002: 14)? Both, no doubt, come into play at the same time and variously, with the audience necessarily divided in its response. On the one hand the laughter identifies the movement – and by extension the performer – as no good; on the other, it suggests an uneasy identification with the performer's limitations and their public experience of humiliation. In other words, the ethics of such laughter can be characterized as exploitative and corrective simultaneously, with the performer positioned as the signifier of fragile, isolated, alienated humanity. But the suspicion remains that this is something of an ideological conjuring trick, produced to dissimulate its real dependence on the structure of commodity fetishism. It is in this connection perhaps worth recalling Bergson's adage that "we laugh every time a person gives us the impression of being a thing" (1980: 97), for thing-like is precisely how the performers are actually being presented. At one point towards the end of the scene, a rather rotund woman responds to the injunction by wobbling her belly up and down enigmatically. The gesture (which, needless to say, produces uproarious laughter), is provocative in that it appears to be both reflecting and resisting the performer's sexualization within the audience's field of vision. This was perhaps the case in the original production, but now, in its second incarnation, the effect is almost the reverse. The audience's laughter objectifies the performance of de-objectification in a manner consistent with the amateur's reification: the woman is made to appear hopelessly unattractive by imitating the nonchalance of "sexy" recalcitrance. And yet she is sexualized nonetheless, caught in the gap between the mimesis of mimesis and the pornography of ordinariness.

The laughing audience is in this respect complicit with the production as a "parody of humanity", and the possibility of identification is maintained only as a "caricature of solidarity" (Adorno and Horkheimer, 1979: 141). The bond between actors and onlookers is as such already highly mediated, the ethical relation being subsumed into a mode of economic circulation. Indeed, the comedy derived from this moment of objectification is consistent with its explicit referencing of the theatre's enactment of exploitation and commodification. The carefully choreographed movement, for all of its seeming spontaneity, appears to separate and detach the woman from her body, presenting it as something she "has" rather than "is", and in the process attempts to reassert her fundamental humanity (Berger, 1997: 46). But the performer in this instance nonetheless appears as a thing, with her belly metonymically reduplicating the body as the centre of her being. Once again the mimetic moment accentuates the distance between the performer and what it is they are performing, demonstrating the alienation of their labour despite the theatrical claim to its "amateur" authenticity. It's as if the self-evidence of the body's historicity, which is here intended to underline the constructedness of the image, returns in the figure of the aged performer as a perverse reminder of its infinite malleability. The attempt to signify individuality at the level of the body thus falls upon the age-old problem of the body's mimetic capacity, whose polyvalence undermines any attempt to inscribe it with the aura of uniqueness (Diamond, 1997: 151). The effect of this is to redouble the sense of the performer's appropriation and alienation, emphasizing further the mimetic quality of the work they are undertaking. In other words, by opening up the gap between "being" and "having" a body, the production reveals a humanist absurdity that the unsuppressed laughter of the audience acknowledges directly. For what appears to be so funny about this moment is not the display of the performer's lack of dexterity or dancerly beauty but in fact the implicit inverse; what is amusing, to me at least, is rather the assumption that this somehow makes them more human, and that the performance of limitation might be considered less inauthentic than the triumph of technique. Is this not a question, finally, of the exposure through laughter of the theatre's barely concealed anthropomorphic fallacy? After all, as Simon Critchley observes, it's less "a person behaving like a thing or vice-versa that is the root of the comic, but rather – surprise surprise – a person acting like a person [sic]. That is, there is something essentially ridiculous about a human being behaving like a human being" (2002: 59). How much more so, then, when the human being's behaviour is deliberately orchestrated to make it seem more human than it might otherwise have been? What difference, in other words, does the labour of the human being as the subject of representation make?

It is worth recalling that this is, essentially, a question of ethics. The trouble with mimesis is precisely the fact that it appears to ground itself in the materiality of the body, but at the same time expropriates it as the vehicle for representation. By articulating itself to an appropriate representative, mimesis is able to function vicariously, and in the process opens the body "itself" to playing a role in something like a drama of infinite "substitution and circulation" (Lacoue-Labarthe, 1989: 116). Mimesis therefore takes on the guise of the human being proper in order to divest it of its "essential" properties, turning adaptability into a mere facet of subjection to economy. In this context, "humanity" exists as just another sign or value to be traded or exchanged with little regard to specificity or utility. And yet, at the same time, the theatrical ethic of representation isn't simply complicit with mimesis' mode of operation: rather than being identical to it, the theatre remains the site of its contestation; rather than simply covering over mimesis-effects or mechanically miming them, performance still offers the opportunity for their exposure or "revelation". The very physicality of the theatrical event – its inhabitation by real bodies – becomes the means by which it is able to identify and define mimesis as being unable to exist on its own without it. Theatrical form in effect demonstrates mimesis to be the mere appearance that it is, opening and closing simultaneously the gap between representation and re-presentation that seems to hold out the promise of alterity. Theatre *sui generis* cannot help but show "what does not present itself and cannot present itself" in its embodiment of action, because "there is represented in it that which has always already represented itself" as the latter's simulation. The attachment of the mimetic to the material is thereby subject to temporalization in the theatre's field of vision, even though their inextricability inevitably remains unaffected. "This is why", as Lacoue-Labarthe says, "there is only one remedy against representation, infinitely precarious, dangerous, and unstable: representation itself" (1989: 117).

The practice of theatre is perhaps approachable, then, as an indefatigable attempt to wrestle with the "timeless" problems mimesis poses. And yet, it might also be suggested, its work is only ever "timely" in that it draws attention to representation's current configuration of the social situation. So the problematic evidenced by the amateur body's commodification is in fact the structurally determining matter of alienation; likewise, the exploitation of the interrelation between intention and technique exposes less the human being's intrinsic limitations than the constraints imposed by the mimesis of mimesis and professionalism of economy. This is a moment of disruption, therefore, that resonates forwards and backwards in time simultaneously. It produces an echo of the freedom that might be imagined to have existed previously, and a call from the future to undertake things differently. The present as such is recreated in this relation, temporalized by the insurgence of history into theatrical form and the emergence through it of the possibility of alterity. Time thereby irrupts into the image, endowing it with the resonance that accompanies the somatic experience of raw laughter and "primordial shudder": an experience, as Adorno says, of "being touched by the other". This surprise occurrence is itself accompanied by a "premonition of subjectivity" sprung upon by the spectator by the indentificatory apparatus of the "mimesis reflex" (Adorno, 1984: 455). According to Adorno, the moment of mimesis' sudden interruption freezes the subject in its tracks: "exposed to a world without world, *before* the world, man likens himself to the immobile nature which surrounds him" [sic]. Nature and the other are in this respect conflated, producing an overwhelming encounter with otherness that is nonetheless "the sign of an opening". This is the opportunity it might seem, then, for a dancerly-type of "self-conservation, self-constitution and self-affirmation" that on the one hand binds the "mimesis reflex" to current reality, and on the other opens out the imaginative space of possibility (Düttmann, 2000: 86–87). Theatrical production might in turn provide the *image* of this "apparition", its manifestation in material form and the temporal site of its occasioning.

Notes

1 Needless to say, it is a man who is left dancing whilst the absent other is, at least figuratively, presumably a woman.
2 Michael Taussig develops an alternative, diametrically opposed conception of mimesis as an "active" rather than passive "yielding" to account for its primary role in the development of a sensuous knowledge of the world and its objects – a mimetic understanding felt in the flesh and sinews of the body (1993: 45–46).
3 These three modes, whilst never stable, are discernible in the different usages of mimesis in Plato and, equally importantly, Aristotle. They are elaborated perhaps most systematically by Paul Ricoeur to account for what he calls "the circle of mimesis" (1990: 46, 52–87).
4 For Agamben, reading Heidegger, potentiality is to be configured as "a capacity that is capable not only of *potentiality* (the manners of Being that are in fact possible) but also, and above all, of *impotentiality*" (1999: 201).
5 This formulation is in fact quite close to the argument advanced by Adorno and Horkheimer, in *Dialectic of Enlightenment* (1979), that mimesis founds an entire project: the instrumentalized domination of nature.

References

Adorno, Theodor W. 1939. 'On Kierkegaard's Doctrine of Love', *Studies in Philosophy and Social Science* 8: 413–429.

Adorno, Theodor W. 1974. *Minima Moralia.* Translated by E. F. N. Jephcott. London. Verso.

Adorno, Theodor W. 1982. 'On the Fetish Character in Music and the Regression of Listening', in Andrew Arato and Eike Gebharddt, eds. *The Essential Fankfurt School Reader.* New York. Continuum.

Adorno, Theodor W. 1984. *Aesthetic Theory.* Edited by G. Adorno and R. Tiedeman, translated by C. Lenhardt. London. Routledge.

Adorno, Theodor W. 1991. *The Culture Industry* Edited by J. M. Bernstein. London and New York. Routledge.

Adorno, Theodor W. 1997. *Aesthetic Theory.* Translated by R. Hullot-Kentor. Minneapolis. University of Minnesota Press.

Adorno, Theodor W. 2002. *The Jargon of Authenticity.* London. Routledge.

Adorno, Theodor W., and Horkheimer, Max. 1979. *Dialectic of Enlightenment.* Translated by J. Cumming. London. Verso.

Agamben, Giorgio. 1998. *Homo Sacer: Sovereign Power and Bare Life.* Translated by D. Heller-Roazen. Stanford. Stanford University Press.

Agamben, Giorgio. 1999. *Potentialities: Collected Essays in Philosophy.* Translated by D. Heller-Roazen. Stanford. Stanford University Press.

Aristotle. 1995. *Poetics.* Edited by Stephen Halliwell. Cambridge, MA. Harvard University Press.

Bayly, Simon. 2002. 'A Pathognomy of Performance: Theatre, Philosophy, and the Ethic of Interruption', unpublished PhD thesis, University of Surrey Roehampton.

Benjamin, Walter. 1978. *Reflections.* Translated by E. Jephcot. New York. Schocken Books.

Berger, John. 1997. *Redeeming Laughter: The Comic Dimension of Human Experience.* Berlin and New York. De Gruyter.

Bergson, Henri. 1980. *Laughter: An Essay on the Meaning of the Comic.* Edited by W. Sypher. Baltimore and London. Johns Hopkins University Press.

Borch-Jacobsen, Mikkel. 1988. *The Freudian Subject.* Translated by C. Porter. Stanford. Stanford University Press.

Borch-Jacobsen, Mikkel. 1991. *Lacan: The Absolute Master.* Translated by D. Brick. Stanford. Stanford University Press.

Critchley, Simon. 2002. *On Humour.* London and New York. Routledge.

Diamond, Elin. 1997. *Unmaking Mimesis: Essays on Feminism and Theater.* New York and London. Routledge.

Düttmann, Alexander Garcia. 2000. *The Gift of Language: Memory and Promise in Adorno, Benjamin, Heidegger and Rosenweig*. Translated by A. Lyons. London. Athlone Press.

Düttmann, Alexander Garcia. 2002. *The Memory of Thought: An Essay on Heidegger and Adorno*. Translated by N. Walker. London and New York. Continuum.

Foreman, Richard. 1992. *Unbalancing Acts: Foundations for a Theater.* New York. Pantheon.

Halliwell, Stephen. 2002. *The Aesthetics of Mimesis: Ancient Texts and Modern Problems.* Princeton and Oxford. Princeton University Press.

Heidegger, Martin. 1977. *Basic Writings.* Edited by David Farrell Krell. San Francisco: HarperCollins.

Heidegger, Martin. 1991. *Nietzsche.* Vol. 4, edited by David Farrell Krell. San Francisco. HarperCollins.

Jameson, Frederic. 1990. *Late Marxism: Adorno, or, The Persistence of the Dialectic*. London. Verso.

Kierkegaard, Søren. 1998. *Works of Love.* Edited and translated by Howard V. Hong and Enda H. Hong. Princeton and Oxford. Princeton University Press.

Lacoue-Labarthe, Philippe. 1998. *Typography: Mimesis, Philosophy, Politics.* Edited by Christopher Fynsk. Stanford. Stanford University Press.

McDonald, William. 2003. 'Love in Kierkegaard's Symposia', *Minerva* 7: 60–93.

Mackrell, Judith. 2002. 'Growing old disgracefully', review of *Kontakthof. The Guardian*, 27 November.

Parry, Jan. 2002. 'There's life in the old legs yet', review of *Kontakthof. The Observer*, 1 December.

Plato. 1961. *The Collected Dialogues.* Edited by E. Hamilton and H. Cairns. New York. Pantheon Books.

Ricoeur, Paul. 1990, *Time and Narrative, Volume 1.* Translated by K. McLoughlin and D. Pellauer. Chicago and London. Chicago University Press.

Ridout, Nicholas. 2000. 'Undecidable Pleasures, or, Who Does Cathy Naden Think She Is?', unpublished paper presented at ASTR 2000, City University of New York.

Rousseau, Jean-Jacques. 1968. *Politics and the Arts: Letter to M. d'Alembert on the Theatre.* Translated by A Bloom. Ithaca. Cornell University Press.

Taussig, Michael. 1993. *Mimesis and Alterity: A Particular History of the Senses.* London and New York. Routledge.

7

CORPSING

John Matthews

Stages of death

There are, as the voice coach Patsy Rodenburg has observed, "many ways to die on stage" (Rodenburg 2002:150). The illustrative examples of the theatricalized deaths of Augustus Caesar and Claire Marshall in Forced Entertainment's *Spectacular* (2008) confirm the veracity of Rodenburg's observation. According to the Roman chronicler Suetonius, on the last day of his life Augustus called for a mirror, had his hair combed and his dropped jaw set straight and, summoning his friends to him, he asked them whether he had played the comedy of life fittingly. His recorded response would suggest that his friends were affirmative: "since the play has been so good, clap your hands and all of you dismiss me with applause" (2000: 95). Though not quite his dying words – these being a rather curt caution to his wife Livia to live mindful of their wedlock – he died shortly after this final performance and presumably with the last reverberations of the sound of applause dying alongside him in his court. By contradistinction, Claire Marshall died her "big death scene" repeatedly in the Riverside Studios, Hammersmith to little applause and diminishing peals of laughter. This theatre company, Forced Entertainment, has experimented with the phenomenon of applause and has been accused by its critics of not giving much to cheer and its particular meditation on the iconography of death in *Spectacular*, where a man in a joke-shop skeleton suit performs alongside a woman perpetually re-enacting a ham cinematic death, is Caesarean only in the sense that it is almost-but-not-quite side-splitting.[1] This word play is not entirely facetious given that, in one etymological sense, the Caesarean recalls the point from which this book started and brings the natal and the fatal into close proximity, associating both with the applause that greets new arrivals and attends on curtain calls.[2] If the applauding audience in the court of Augustus Caesar had little cause to doubt the authenticity of his "spectacular" death then the audience in the Riverside Studios were given no cause to imagine the spectacle they witnessed to be authentic. Perhaps, in response to Rodenburg's observation, the distinction between my two examples is a little too stark – only one after all is a *real* death and only one occurred on a *real* stage. The spectacle of Augustus' death was constructed on the stage of his power as Caesar but this is not, of course, the kind of stage to which Rodenburg refers: Rodenburg is writing about the many different ways *theatrical characters* die – stabbed, stoned, suffocated in cupboards, thrown from windows etc – and the dramaturgical considerations of each. In yet another passage I cannot help but read ironically, Rodenburg claims:

> there are usually two main concerns connected with dying: the death speech and after death, lying on the stage dead but without the audience seeing you breathing. (2002: 150)

Whilst my ironic reading has much to do with my own (deficient) sense of humour it is not altogether irrelevant given that the ambiguity inherent in Rodenburg's statements about death and dying actually relates to the particularly theatrical conditions of dying, both on and off stage.

On a "genuine" theatrical stage Marshall's death was carefully represented so as to convey, quite unambiguously, that is was not in fact death, or even dying. As with all acts of representation, it was simultaneously its fidelity to and disparity from the thing it represented which enabled it to achieve its particular affect. If the stage on which Augustus dies is not technically the kind of stage to which Rodenburg refers then the "reality", which is to say biological actuality, of his death is also not technically the kind of death to which she would like to draw our attention. That said, the representational qualities operative in both Ancient Rome and present day London have generated some memorable and quite spectacular "death scenes", some of which bring into relief the ethical attitudes inscribed in current dying conduct.

Just as there are many ways to die on stage there are also, as Allan Kellehear has written, many *stages* of death. In one sense, these *stages* of death refer to historical *ages* – "stone" age, "pastoral" age, the "age of the city", the "cosmopolitan age" (Kellehear, 2007: vii) – proceeding from the "dawn of mortal awareness" until the present. Each of these historical ages is, according to Kellehear, characterized by an attitudinal shift in relation to death and dying. In a sense pertinent to the theatrical, *stages of death* also refer to the specific organization of "structural patterns", "preparations", "rites" and "behaviour" (2007: 16) which codify attitudes towards dying in any given historical age. Kellehear's work on *The Social History of Dying* has shown that the management of these stages, not of *death* per se but rather of the *experience of dying*, are socially inscribed and iterated. The biological episode of death has long been stage-managed as a sociocultural and psychological event of "dying", which, like "the theatre", operates as a site for community "meaning-making" (2007: 16).[3] The reasons why we die as we do today, what Kellehear calls "current dying conduct" (2007: 16), have comparatively little to do with the biological episode of death and much more to do with epidemiology, economics, religion and moral philosophy. Our current dying conduct has built up incrementally over thousands of years and as such, mapped within our contemporary *stages of dying* is the latest set of ethical coordinates for living. Having taken some licence with Rodenburg's observation and compared the experience of "playing dead" with the playfulness of dying I propose to examine one famous "death in play" in this chapter in order to discuss some normative ethics encoded in contemporary dying conduct.

The way we conduct ourselves is a matter of *performance* or, as Nicholas Ridout (2009) has expressed it, a question of *how to act*. Assessing the normative ethics of contemporary dying conduct entailed in actions – and attitudes about those actions – in proximity to death requires some historical focus on performance and ethical philosophy in this chapter. This chapter unpicks some of the ethics evinced in actions and attitudes in the performance of dying through the particular framework of "corpsing" and what Jure Gantar has called "the inherent ethical ambivalence of laughter" (2005: 5).

No laughing matter

Laughter and death are closely associated in popular parlance relating to staged performance as well as in the theatrical vernacular: "laughing" and "dying" are almost synonyms in the context of statements made about comedians "slaying" an audience, or in the now popular refrain, "you're killing me!". "I laughed so hard, I almost died" could serve as another example of the quasi-synonymous relation between death and laughter. In the colloquial speech of theatre, and increasingly television, laughter and death are bound together under the sign of "the corpse". In theatre, to "corpse" is to break character, specifically by laughing inappropriately and, whilst the origins of the term "corpsing" are unknown, popular myth has it that it derives from the practice of trying to make one's fellow actors laugh whilst lying, apparently dead, on stage. The notion that such a practice might be so widespread in theatre as to inspire specific terminology is appealing (to my sense of humour) but, without taking folklore for historical fact, part of its appeal derives from its credibility – "the theatre" is, after all, full of dead bodies: notable examples include Antigone's beloved Polynices, Dario Fo's "the anarchist", all three children of Bertolt Brecht's Mother Courage, Arthur Miller's Willy Loman, Brendan Behan's Leslie Williams in *The Hostage,* Athol Fugard's Sizwe Bansi, Wole Soyinka's horseman and, perhaps amongst the most famous stiffs-on-stage, Hamlet and Son. On stages so cluttered with corpses, and for actors so frequently prostrate "animating" them, there is something appealingly apposite in the professional necessity of cultivating a practice of "corpsing". The practice, or art, of corpsing as well as the contemporary usage of the term to denote inappropriate laughter rather begs the question, "what is so funny about death?" or, to rephrase in less rhetorical terms, "why is death so funny?"

It should be clear that, at a profound level, death is not funny at all. Death can be deeply upsetting, and yet laughter often attends on death. This laughter can come in several forms or "typologies" to use Jure Gantar's word.[4] Laughter and tears frequently arise together – the philosopher Francis Bacon was probably not the first to note that joy can put a sparkle in the eye and "sometimes tears" (1627 [1996]: 96). Just as we can "cry happy tears" we can also laugh uncontrollably during fits of distress and the well-established theatrical genre of tragicomedy has been capitalizing on this oxymoronic relation for some time.[5] Given our proclivity for "matrixing" all stage events into the narrative of performance – Ridout has noted that the stage alone is sufficient in "producing the illusion of intention" (2006: 102) – it is unsurprising that biological deaths on stage have often been read by audiences as having occurred *within* the fictional world of the performance. The death on stage of comedic performer Sid James has entered folklore because of the poignancy of the spectacle of his death, caused by the attendance of laughter upon it. The later public demise of his contemporary, Eric Morecombe, on stage in Tewkesbury on 28 May 1984, has attained perhaps a doubly affecting poignancy as a result of the simultaneous occurrence of laughter *and* applause – Morecombe died leaving the stage after his sixth curtain call and shortly after reporting his fear of dying in the manner of his friend, Tommy Cooper, to the audience. Cooper's death on stage remains the most iconic of the modern era – Molière's death as the Hypochondriac perhaps the most iconic of an earlier age – and the one to which all other such collapses are related, because of the simple fact that it was viewed by almost 50,000 people.

Centre stage, in front of the meeting point of two red velvet curtains with gold brocade trim, Cooper stood at the microphone. Behind the curtains, Cooper's back-stage assistant for "the magic coat skit", Jimmy Tarbuck, was waiting to hand through the gap and into Cooper's coat a range of props, progressively increasing in size from a paint pot to a step ladder. Cooper would appear to pull them from inside his "magic coat" until, at the last, Tarbuck would come through his legs with the stepladder. Cooper signalled to his on-stage assistant to bring him his "magic coat". From stage left, she approached Cooper with his magic coat, she helped him on with it, loosely buttoning up the front and turned to take the microphone stand off stage. As she did so, Cooper, arms outstretched as if ready to deliver his famous "just like that" catchphrase, slumped downwards to the floor with his knees awkwardly buckled under him. The crowd began to laugh, even

Cooper's on-stage assistant looked back and smiled as she took the microphone stand to the wings – "he was a real terror for introducing new bits and pieces without warning" Tarbuck later explained (Bevan, 2009).

Cooper sat on his haunches with his chin on his chest producing the effect of amplifying his laboured breathing through the microphone attached to his shirt for nearly ten seconds. Then, with inadvertent comic timing, his body fell backwards and part way through the gap in the curtains – a roar of laughter from the audience. At this point Tarbuck realized "something terrible had happened" and called for a commercial break. Several seconds of blank screen were broadcast to the audience as London Weekend Television's master control contacted regional stations to notify them to start transmitting adverts.

Cooper's collapse during the live TV performance broadcast from Her Majesty's Theatre didn't stop the show – this must, evidently, go on. Though reports vary, and much myth-making has gone on, it is true that some of Cooper's fellow performers delivered their acts on the forestage in front of the closed curtain while paramedics sought to revive Cooper, who was barely concealed behind it. Two acts, the duo Les Dennis and Dustin Gee and the singer Howard Keel, performed thus but, with the imminent arrival on stage of Donny Osmond and a 24-strong dancing troupe, Cooper's body had to be stretchered away. Reports that Cooper's famously large feet protruded underneath the curtain and on to the forestage during those two acts do not seem credible – though the host for that evening, Jimmy Tarbuck, claimed in a recent interview with *Wales on Sunday* that, "he was a big bloke and very heavy; we just couldn't move him [backstage]" (Bevan, 2009) – but they do perhaps evoke the atmosphere that must have persisted in Her Majesty's Theatre for the remainder of the performance.

In the event of Cooper's death, and the immediate and subsequent response to it, certain dimensions of contemporary dying conduct are drawn into relief and these are associated with the ethical codes directing the behaviour of the living. I would suggest that the legendary "red curtain" of the theatre has never been so appositely used to simultaneously prohibit and excite the gaze of an audience, or iconographically to signal an end to performance. Whilst the curtain here may be redolent of the no-less-iconic blanket used to cover the deceased, it is really the blanket that takes its power from a theatrical economy of sight and blindness. Blindness in this context is, of course, not total blindness: we can, we *must* look on the dead but we must do so through any one of a number of epidermises from blankets, to caskets, body-bags and flags. In the example of Cooper's collapse the operations of the most iconic of all modern epidermises, the TV screen, lays bare the fraught ethics of sight and blindness, and laughter, at the intersection of life and death.

Communications technology has revived the age-old ethical question of censorship: though Cooper's collapse was broadcast live, the broadcasters of the show from Her Majesty's Theatre, London Weekend Television (LWT), took the decision not to broadcast the footage again. However, footage of Cooper's collapse was leaked onto the Internet site YouTube in early May 2009 and has, at the point of writing, been viewed by more people than saw the live broadcast.[6] Despite calls from many quarters, including the Tory MP Philip Davies, sitting on the Commons Culture, Media and Sport Select Committee, for the footage to be removed – as other "offensive" video clips that violate YouTube's "Community Guidelines"[7] have been removed – YouTube did not delete the posting. Davies, speaking to Chris Irvine of *The Telegraph*, contended that "most people would find that [the footage] tasteless" (Irvine, 2009) and, implying that the footage should be removed said, "they [YouTube] ought to have some regard to his family".

Understanding exactly why it is "tasteless" to watch another human being die is not as easy as one might at first suspect. The account of the death of Augustus Caesar suggests that spectating on death has not always been ethically problematic and there are many cultures, including my own European one, in which spectating on death has, at times, been regarded as almost a civic responsibility – Foucault's writings on the public executions are one salutary reminder of this fact.[8] Despite the evidence offered by Augustus Caesar and Michel Foucault to suggest that looking on death might, in certain social and historical contexts be, to quote the catchphrase of Cooper's contemporary Kenny Everett, "in the best possible taste", spectating on Cooper's collapse remains problematic because of the disparity between the *theatricalization* of this collapse and the structures of a *theatre of* contemporary dying conduct.

Certain dimensions of the theatre of contemporary dying conduct can be witnessed in the formalization of behaviour around death in hospitals. The so-called Liverpool Care Pathway – a "best practice model" used to "drive up sustained quality of dying in the last hours and days of life" – provides one protocol of behaviour around the dying. This protocol, designed to delimit both medical treatment and guide the "spiritual" care of patients and families, reiterates some of the cherished and implicit values of contemporary society about conduct around death and formalizes behaviours that had already sedimented into standard practices in hospitals: for example, unnecessary speaking is minimized amongst medical practitioners attending the family of a terminal patient and quiet or silence maintained around them. Privacy for a patient's family is prioritized and hospitals offer rooms or curtains (more examples of the aforementioned epidermises) to enclose a family group once a patient is "on the pathway".

Part of the ethical problem with watching footage of Cooper's death is associated with *who* is watching it. In contrast to the private and familial context of idealized dying conduct in hospitals, this death is now *public* in the most expansive twenty-first-century definition of the word (the online polis or "community"). Davies' claim that "everybody knows he [Cooper] died on stage. I don't think we need to see this to be reminded of that" (Irvine, 2009) seems somewhat disingenuous – it seems unlikely that he imagines that viewers of the video are solely seeking to confirm the truthfulness of accounts surrounding Cooper's death. The impulse to view the footage – the impulse that Davies finds so abhorrent – is rather a very literal manifestation of what is commonly called *morbid curiosity*.

One historical lineage of the contemporary disapproval of morbid curiosity might have something to do with the notion of contagion – the capacity we exhibit for being influenced by what we see. It was this capacity, intimately bound up in the question of mimesis, that first caused Plato to banish theatre from his idealized Republic, and thus the ethics of contagion have always been, in one sense, a question of theatre.[9] Morbid curiosity is a phenomenon especially linked to theatre in its earliest modern guise – the museum of anatomy. As Romanyshyn writes, the "cultural connection between the corpse and the stage" (1989: 119) has a long history not least because the first mention of the sale of a ticket to a public anatomy comes in 1497, establishing a precedent, according to William Heckscher, followed by the first playhouses which were to be constructed almost a century later (Heckscher, 1958). Even in this earliest historical manifestation, entrance into the theatre of the corpse has been stringently policed. Beginning with the Anatomy Theatre, reserved for medical practitioners and students, the anatomy museums were initially accessible only to gentlemen. According to Michael Sappol, curator at the National Library of Medicine, Bethesda, outrage at these anatomy museums was, as Davies put it centuries later, a matter of "taste". Much like the voyeuristic display of home movies uploaded to YouTube and similar sites, the anatomy museum was an "institution devoted to the display of things that should not be displayed" (Sappol, 2004). The policing of access to anatomy museums, and their ultimate closure by law in the 1930s, was largely motivated by the belief that far from edifying those who entered, they corrupted. In words that paraphrase Davies' criticism of the YouTube video, a *Boston Medical and Surgical Journal* editorial of July 24, 1873 denounced "Dr Jourdain's Gallery of Anatomy" for displaying "representations . . . most improper for public exhibition" (Sappol, 2004). The impropriety of these representations was in part associated with the financial exploitation of visitors by "quack" doctors who would sell snake oil remedies (or quacksalves, in sixteenth-century parlance) to visitors but also associated with the capacity to "excite the morbid curiosity of the young" and to induce "peculiar forms of hypochondria" (ibid). The "harm" brought about by exposure to such representations, one editor of the Boston journal noted, "cannot be calculated" (ibid).

The ethically transgressive and morally corrupting effects of the public anatomies direct theatre philosophy back to what are often regarded as its roots: Aristotle's recuperation of the theatre into society, following Plato's banishment of it, initiating over two centuries of argumentation over theatre's ethical capabilities and responsibilities. Morbid curiosity is deeply bound to theatre, not only because of the historical connections between playhouses and anatomy museums and the interpersonal dynamics of the *theatron* – the voyeurism of what Patrick Campbell has described as a "division between disembodied seer and blind embodied actor" (2001: 32) – but also because morbid curiosity is the guiding principle of many of the more iconic narratives of the theatre. The morbid curiosity of a theatre audience that *must see what happens* is often parallelled by the morbid curiosity of a protagonist *who must know the truth*: Hamlet's impatience to discover the truth of the King's murder from his father's ghost – "haste, haste me to know it" (Act 1 Scene VI) – sets him on an ill-fated course of revenge just as Oedipus' insatiable desire to discover the cause of the Theban plague drives him to his own destruction. Not only is there something potentially harmful and (morally) corrupting about morbid curiosity, it is also "improper" because its insatiable appetite does not respect boundaries. All ethics have cartography; ethics always specifies not only what we should and should not do, or ask, but also where we should and should not go, or even, look. However, the ethics of dying conduct exposed by the outrage attending on Internet footage of Cooper's collapse is not just about spectation; not just about an audience and *vision* but also about audience and *sound*.

Respect

Davies does not appear to disapprove of the laughter of the live theatre audience in Her Majesty's Theatre as such. Their laughter is *innocent*, a physiological response prompted by the organization of stage events.[10] There is nothing *wrong* with their laughter but, as Gantar has shown,

> Just because we think there is nothing wrong with laughter as a physiological reaction, we should not automatically assume that all laughter is by definition ethical. (Gantar, 2005: 32)

Situating laughter within the historical development of ethical philosophy, Jure Gantar traces a prejudice against laughter through Christian discourse back to the fourth century. She makes a case for an historical and accumulative philosophical prejudice against laughter starting with Aristotle's association of the ludicrous with the ugly and the bad, and continuing into the present day. Gantar argues that the "most drastic philosophical denunciations of laughter" can be found in the writings of seventeenth century Puritans and in so doing aligns her "history of laughter" (2005: 5) with the canonical history of theatre: Aristotle's poetics being the point of initiation for both a hegemonic theatre-history and a prejudice against laugher, and the seventeenth century being a significant moment within both histories for the wholesale emergence of the professional theatre and the simultaneous enumeration of both plays and treatise on the moral repugnance of laughter.[11]

According to Gantar, the critical treatment of laughter "has never suffered from a lack of ethical, moral, or even moralistic principles" (2005: 4). Laughter, according to Wayne C. Booth in his investigation into the role of ethics in literary criticism, has, as a common audience response, been seen to have "an ethical edge to it" (Booth, 1988: 310). As far back as the Renaissance critics, such as the Italian scholar Lodovico Castelvetro, asserted that we laugh because "we assume that we are superior [to the subject of our laughter]" (Gantar, 2005: 7). The power of laughter to set divisions is a tool of the satirist and, at various points in the history of theatre, humour – as a rhetorical device belonging to comedy – has been excluded from "proper" theatre because of what John Dryden called "the *malicious* pleasure of the audience which is testified to by laughter" (Gantar, 2005: 19, my italics). Whilst laughter can forge alliances – what is popularly called laughing *with* someone as opposed to laughing *at* them – laughter can also place us above the object of our laughter. Laughter can be judgemental and wounding; as Konrad Lorenz argued, "laughter can turn into a very cruel weapon if it strikes a defenceless human being undeservedly" (2002: 284). It is perhaps Cooper's vulnerability in this footage, the exposure of his mortal frailty that makes laughing at his collapse – or rather endorsing the laughter attending on his collapse by re-viewing it – so reprehensible to Davies. The wounding power of laughter, Lorenz asserts, places a moral responsibility on the amused to *not laugh* at the vulnerable generating inviolable moral laws such as "it is criminal to laugh at a child" (ibid). It is, however, perhaps more than the divisive and judgemental force of laughter that makes the scene of Cooper's death so problematic.

Laughter foregrounds difference between the laugher and the laughed at, and in the matter of dying we are made forcibly aware of our sameness: death is, as we all know, one of a small number of common human experiences. In this context laughter might be a reasonable response – one might want to foreground the distinction between life and death to give more comfort to the living – but it is also a nonsensical one. Laughter as a response to death is nonsensical, and thus perhaps distasteful, in other ways too. Laughter, like death, cannot be controlled. It is excessive. In contrast, all dying conduct constructs highly controlled, highly theatricalized rites around death. The theatre of dying conduct is typified by its controlled organization of conduct around death and in the theatre of dying conduct the excessiveness of laughter is an unwelcome reminder of our absolute subjection to the caprice of mortality.

Laughter is not only excessive, it is arbitrary; its appearance is determined by chance, whim or impulse and is grounded only in the preferences or judgements of individuals. Like other arbitrary events and principles, "laughter undermines any kind of structure, including the structures of ethics and morality" (Gantar, 2005: 151). As such, laughter is a phenomenon that "defies the mere possibility of ethics" (152). Accordingly, in its emergence at a moment in which ethical attitudes are manifested in highly orchestrated and ritualized behavioural codes, its destabilizing presence might be unwelcome. The malicious intent of laughter, to quote Dryden, and its excessive and arbitrary character make it an ethically problematic phenomenon in the context of death conduct because death is something that commands our *respect*.

> This is very poor taste. That the broadcasters [LWT] have not repeated the incident shows they have a respect for him [Cooper] and I think that ought to apply also on YouTube. They [YouTube] should take it all down out of respect for Mr Cooper and his remaining family.

The above statement is taken from an article in *The Daily Mail*. John Beyer from Mediawatch UK (a pressure group founded in the 1960s by the late Mary Whitehouse) uses the term "respect" twice here to substantiate his argument that the Internet footage of Cooper's collapse should be removed. Respect, as a philosophical concept, is closely allied to the perhaps even more slippery term, "dignity". Dignity crops up recurrently in contemporary discourse on euthanasia, which is increasingly fighting its way to the fore at the moment.[12] Whether the sovereign dignity of Life trumps the pain and suffering of terminal illness or whether prolonged palliative care infringes dignity so that "assisted suicide" becomes an ethically preferable option is a hotly contested question at present. In the contexts of these questions "dignity" becomes increasingly ineffable and the more (philosophically) pedestrian concept of "respect" often supplants it. Beyer's assertion that viewing or not viewing Tommy Cooper's dying is a matter of "respect" finally draws this analysis of laughter and dying conduct firmly within the realm of the moral philosophy of ethics. Speculating on the historical development of the idea that all human persons as such deserve respect, Feinburg identifies three distinct concepts denoted by the term "respect".[13] Anchoring his thesis in Kant's writings on *Achtung* (a German word which, in the context of Kant's writing, is usually translated as "respect"), Feinburg argues that "respect" encompasses three distinct attitudes towards things. First, *respekt* is that "uneasy and watchful attitude that has an 'element of fear' in it" (1975: 1) and this is accorded to things which endanger or hold power over the subject. Secondly, *observantia* which, according to Feinburg, encompasses that which is now generally regarded as owed to all humans equally by virtue of their being human, as well as the deference which acknowledges different social positions. Thirdly, *reverentia* is the feeling of awe that we find in the presence of the sublime. This is perhaps most memorably expressed in Kant's account of the moral law and people who exemplify it: this law, and those who exemplify it, command *reverentia* because we experience these as that which "always trumps our inclinations in determining our wills" (Feinburg, 1975: 2). It is in the matter of "determining our will", against the power of our own inclinations, that respect tracks onto ethical codes in the realm of dying conduct. Whilst attitudes of respect can be held without manifesting in action, respect is generally thought to be an expression of agency and to have a behavioural component that is "object-generated". We respect something because we recognize that we *have to* (Wood, 1999); it involves a "deontic experience" – the experience that one must pay attention and *act* appropriately (Birch, 1993). It is generally taken that a principle of respect is that it prescribes the actions that express it (Frankena, 1986; Downie and Telfer, 1969) and it is, in this way, associated with "appropriate conduct".[14] Perhaps death, or dying, commands all three forms of respect: it is, as Socrates noted, the experience that *all* men (irrationally) fear most (Plato, *Apology*: 29a).[15] It is a nodal point in our shared experience of humanity and death, or dying, is awe inspiring in the true sense of the term and quite emphatically "trumps our inclinations" despite the best efforts of modern medicine and the health industry.

"Respect", from the Latin *respicere,* "to look back at", has a sensorial dimension and is allied to the philosophical notion of an *imperative*, which also has a particular association with Kant, and moral philosophy. Events, objects and experiences which command a certain response are not uncommonly associated with the senses: another example of yielding to an imperative from beyond the subject could be found in the religious experience of "vocation", from the Latin *vocare*, "to call". As Beyer points out, our conduct around death is a matter of behaving ethically. This is because death, Cooper's death in this instance, commands our respect; commands us to behave in certain ways and this command is stronger than our wills. The ambiguity of theatrical representation and the latent potential for matrixing all stage events into the narrative of performance complicates this command: death might command a certain "respectful" response from us but so does theatre.

I am not talking about "respect" in the somewhat moribund sense summoned by works with titles such as *Respect For Acting* (1973) wherein we are invited to "give theatre its due" but about respect as a deontic phenomenon, as that principle which prescribes the action that expresses it. Much theatre scholarship in the wake of Erving Goffman's *Presentation of Self in Everyday Life* (1959) and *Frame Analysis* (1974) has shown us that the theatrical experience is scripted in the widest possible sense of the term. "Performances", Keir Elam tells us, "can be properly understood only on the basis of theatrical competence, *more or less shared by performers and audiences*" (2002: 78, emphasis added) and theatrical events are distinguished from other events – such as, for example, the event of dying – according to organizational and cognitive principles which, "like all cultural rules, have to be learnt" (ibid). The cognitive component of the theatrical event is uniquely problematic since the "most fundamental form of competence required before the spectator can begin to decode the text [i.e. performance] appropriately" is "the ability to recognize the performance *as such*" (ibid). The laughing of the live audience in Her Majesty's Theatre is a manifest *incompetence* but is not opprobrious because it is *erroneous* and not *malicious*; malice requires intent. The failure of the live audience to recognize this performance *as such*, which in this case is perhaps to say *not as such*, arises because of a combination of the strictly rule-governed conduct proscribed in theatre and the inherent ambiguity of theatrical spectacle – as I mentioned at the outset, its *fidelity to* and *disparity from* the thing it represented. It is, by contrast, precisely the competence of the YouTube audience, their capacity to view the performance *as such* that draws disapproval. The fact that one matrixed dimension of the performance is the laughter of the live audience is ethically problematic because it is now, in a sense, taken "out of context". The laughing of the live audience is regrettable but excusable whilst the representation of this laughter matrixed within a new online spectacle of dying wilfully violates the behavioural codes laid down by that which trumps our wills; death. The matrixing of laughter within this example of dying conduct draws the "ethically ambivalent" force of laughter to the centre of an event from which it should be properly evacuated. In the constructed event of the YouTube performance the ethically ambivalent force of laughter can be contrasted with the ethically decisive statement of applause operative in Augustus' death. Returning to the assertion that instigated this chapter, we can perhaps agree that, whilst there are many ways to die on stage, some are more tasteful than others.

Notes

1 Numerous commentators have described Forced Entertainment's work as boring and the *Guardian* theatre critic Lyn Gardener – actually one of their more vocal supporters – has noted that "they have turned boredom into an art form" (Gardener 2008).

2 The etymology of the term "caesarean section" is difficult to trace and the connection between the practice and Julius Caesar is likely to be an anachronism. One (unsubstantiated) theory about the origin of the term asserts that it derives from a Roman legal code, 'Lex Caesarea' which allegedly entailed that a child be cut from the mother's womb in the event of her death during labour (see England & Horowitz, 1998: 159). Another more popular theory relies on the story told by Pliny the Elder in the first century AD which claims that an ancestor of Caesar was delivered by being cut from his mother's womb (Pliny, 1949–1962). An alternative, and perhaps most likely, etymology holds that the term derives from the Latin verb *caedere* meaning 'to cut' though a supposed historical connection with Caesar would appear to have influenced the spelling at some point in history and this connection is borne out by the fact that the German, Danish, Dutch, Hungarian (*Kaiserschnitt*, *kejsersnit*, *keizersnede* and *császármetszés* respectively) terms all translate as "emperor's cut".

3 As Marvin Carlson has written an "affective starting point for the intersection of new theory and performance is almost invariably located within a study of meaning-making and the emergence of semiotics in the late 1960s and 1970s" (Carlson in Reinelt and Roach, 1992: 13)

4 Gantar's collection of typologies of laughter includes numerous literary sources: Baudelaire, for example, differentiates between "significative" and "absolute" laughter; Marcel Pagnol between "positive" and "negative"; Etienne Sourieau between "crude" and "comic"; Ernest Dupréel between "the laughter of welcome" and "the laughter of exclusion" and Herbert Blau between the uncontrollable laughter associated with the comedy of the absurd and the decisively inferior "pallid laughter of amnesia" (Gantar, 2005: 32).

5 See Carrington-Lancaster (2009: ix).

6 Statistics taken from YouTube.com and accurate at time of first publication.

7 Full details of YouTube community guidelines can be found at youtube.com/t/community_guidelines but some of the "common sense rules" stated here include: "YouTube is not for pornography", "Don't post videos showing things like animal abuse, drug abuse or bomb-making", "graphic or gratuitous violence is not allowed" and "don't post disgusting videos of accidents, dead bodies and similar things".
8 See *Discipline and Punish* chapter 1 'The Body of the Condemned'.
9 See Plato. *The Republic,* Books II, III and X.
10 The assumption here demands some comment: I have described this response as physiological but there are no doubt critics who might want to emphasize the conscious conformity to behavioural codes in this context. The contention is that within the instructive framework of the comic performance laughter remains an involuntary response in spite of the voluntary participation of the individual with the social framework.
11 Examples of seventeenth-century texts in which laughter is associated with "atheism, immorality and disorderliness" include Jeremy Collier's *Short View of the Immorality and Profaneness of the English Stage* (1698); Joseph Granvill's *A Whip for the Droll, Fiddler to the Atheist* (1668) and *Seasonable Reflections and Discourses to the Conviction and Cure of Scoffing and Infidelity of a Degenerate Age* (1676) and Clement Ellis's *Vanity of Scoffing* (1674) and *The Gentile Sinner* (1660) (Gantar, 2005: 6).
12 A suitably performative and topical example of discourse on dignity and dying can be located in the recent television drama written by Irish playwright Frank McGuinness, *A Short Stay in Switzerland* (BBC 2009), based on the life Dr Anne Turner who made headlines in 2006 when she travelled to a so-called "suicide clinic" in Zurich after being diagnosed with an incurable neurological disease.
13 Hudson (1980) proposes four categories of respect: *evaluative* respect; *obstacle* respect; *directive* respect and *institutional* respect while Dillon (1992) adds a fifth category: *care* respect, which is that given to an object believed to have profound and unique value. Darwall (1977) isolates only two categories of respect: *recognition* respect and *appraisal* respect but this chapter draws primarily on Feinburg's three typologies because of the focus these classifications place on the power of the respect-worthy objection to command our attention and *direct our actions* and, in the context of *performance* and ethics, and especially dying *conduct,* action is integral.
14 See Buss (1999) for disagreement.
15 Plato attributes the famous argument that fear of death is irrational to Socrates, asserting that whilst no mortal being can have knowledge of death "all men fear it as if they knew for certain it is the greatest evil" (2002: 29a).

References

Bacon, F. 1627 [1996]. *Sylva Sylavrum, or, A Natural History in Ten Centuries.* Kessinger.

Bevan, N. 2009. 'Tommy Cooper's Last Act Fooled Us All Says Jimmy Tarbuck,' *Wales on Sunday* (12 April). Online at http://www.walesonline.co.uk/news/

wales-news/2009/04/12/tommy-cooper-s-last-act-fooled-us-all-says-jimmy-tarbuck-91466-23367910/ – accessed 5 January 2010.

Birch, T. H. 1993. 'Moral Considerability and Universal Consideration,' *Environmental Ethics* 15: 313–332.

Booth, W. C. 1988. *The Company We Keep: An Ethics of Fiction.* Berkeley, CA and London. University of California Press.

Buss, S. 1999. 'Respect for Persons,' *Canadian Journal of Philosophy* 29: 517–550.

Campbell, P. (ed.). 2001. *The Body in Performance.* London and New York. Routledge.

Carrington-Lancaster, H. 2009. *The French Tragi-comedy.* Charleston, SC. Bibliobazaar.

Darwall, S. 1977. 'Two Kinds of Respect,' *Ethics* 88: 36–49.

Dillon, R. S. 1992. 'Respect and Care: Toward Moral Integration,' *Canadian Journal of Philosophy* 22: 105–132.

Downie, R. S., and Telfer, E. 1969. *Respect for Persons.* London. George Allen and Unwin.

Elam, K. 2002. *The Semiotics of Theatre and Drama.* London and New York. Routledge.

England, P., and Horowitz, R. I. 1998. *Birthing from Within: An Extra-ordinary Guide to Childbirth Preparation.* Alberquerque, NM. Patera Press.

Feinburg, J. 1975. 'Some Conjectures on the Concept of Respect,' *Journal of Social Philosophy* 4: 1–3.

Foucault, M. 1975 [1991]. *Discipline and Punish.* London. Penguin Books.

Frankena, W. K. 1986. 'The Ethics of Respect for Persons,' *Philosophical Topics* 14: 149–167.

Gantar, J. 2005. *The Pleasure of Fools: Essays in the Ethics of Laughter.* Kingston, ON. McGill-Queens Press.

Gardner, L. 2008. 'Forced Entertainment: The Theatre Company that Refuses to Grow Old,' *The Guardian* (23 February).

Goffman, E. 1959. *The Presentation of Self in Everyday Life.* New York. Doubleday Anchor.

Goffman, E. 1974. *Frame Analysis: An Essay on the Organisation of Experience.* Boston, MA. Northeastern University Press.

Hagen, U. 1973. *Respect for Acting.* Trans. H. Frankel. Oxford. Wiley.

Heckscher, W. S. 1958. *Rembrandt's Anatomy of Dr Nicolaas Tulp.* New York. New York University Press.

Hudson, S. D. 1980. 'The Nature of Respect,' *Social Theory and Practice* 6: 69–90.

Irvine, C. 2009. 'Footage of Tommy Cooper's Death on Stage Shown on YouTube,' *Daily Telegraph* (9 May). Online at http://www.telegraph.co.uk/technology/news/5298541/Footage-of-Tommy-Coopers-death-on-stage-shown-on-YouTube.html – accessed 5 January 2010.

Kellehear, A. 2007. *A Social History of Dying.* Cambridge. Cambridge University Press.

'Liverpool Care Pathway.' http://www.liv.ac.uk/mcpcil/liverpool-care-pathway/ – accessed 5 January 2010.

Lorenz, K. 2002. *On Aggression.* London and New York. Routledge.

Plato. 2002. *Five Dialogues.* Trans. G. M. A. Grube. Indianapolis, IN. Hackett.

Pliny. 1949–1962. *Natural History.* Trans. H. Rackham et al. Cambridge, MA. Harvard University Press.

Reinelt, J., and Roach, J. 2007. *Critical Theory and Performance.* Ann Arbor, MI. University of Michigan Press.

Revoir, P. 2009. 'YouTube Storm over Video Showing Tommy Cooper's Death on Stage,' *Daily Mail* (9 May). Online at http://www.dailymail.co.uk/tvshowbiz/ article–1179569/YouTube-storm-video-showing-tommy-cooper-death-stage.html – accessed 5 January 2010.

Ridout, N. 2006. *Stage Fright: Animals and other Theatrical Problems.* Cambridge. Cambridge University Press.

Ridout, N. 2009. *Theatre and Ethics.* London and Basingstoke. Palgrave Macmillan.

Rodenburg, P. 2002. *The Actor Speaks: Voice and the Performer.* London and Basingstoke. Palgrave Macmillan.

Romanyshyn, R. D. 1989. *Technology as Symptom and Dream.* London. Routledge.

Sappol, M. 2004. 'Morbid Curiosity: The Decline and Fall of the Popular Anatomical Museum,' *Common Place* 4(2). Online at http://www.historycoperative._org/ journals/cp/vol-04/no-02/sappol/ – accessed 5 January 2010.

Suetonius. 2000. *The Lives of the Caesars.* Trans. C. Edwards. Oxford. Oxford University Press.

Wood, A. W. 1999. *Kant's Ethical Thought.* Cambridge. Cambridge University Press.

8

THE SENSE OF AN ENDING: NOTES FOR BEGINNERS

Alan Read

Closing Time[1]

The theatre, by which I mean that traffic of "the illuminated stage", comes to an end.[2] This should not go without saying before we finish. Indeed, this is saying something quite different to the various complex "ontologies" of performance where that traffic is figured as ephemeral, as disappearing, as unrepeatable, all those ghostings that have come to define the melancholic fixation of theatre's sister act, performance study. We know the theatre comes to an end because we watch the people we thought we knew for a while take a bow and leave, before we leave. And we do go, despite the inclination to stay just where we are. We leave quite rapidly, irrespective of how decent the show was, and we leave as closely as we can to the others who are leaving despite our best intentions to tarry awhile. Gaps in aisles are surreptitiously filled. It is not quite as bad as Richard Yates' forensic formulation of theatrical disappointment at the outset of his novel *Revolutionary Road*: "When the curtain fell at last it was an act of mercy". But it is still quite brutal. There is little love lost in departure from a spent auditorium.

Or is there? Is there a way to consider further this sense of an ending and the love lost right there? Quite how it feels and how much of it there is that has been lost? Richard Yates offers us an anatomy of such departures and figures everything that follows in his celebrated novel. Upon the way a shattered, bewildered gaggle of individuals, who before this night had imagined themselves some sort of community, find their way to leave each other, in the auditorium, in the parking lot, under stars that Dante might, if he had lived in a Connecticut suburb, have offered as the canopy for a *Divine Comedy*. But the fiction at work that follows this theatrical alienation dwarfs the modest beginnings from which its ends arise. The theatre may end but Yates weaves his literary workings in the rubble of its epilogue as though as to remind us that an act of mercy in a theatrical ending may be the cruel prologue to something much more interminable.

We know the phenomenology of this literary counterpart to theatre's ending that has operated as a beginning, a stage on which everything else beyond theatre is about to be played out. It, the book, or perhaps more felicitously the volume, feels heavy in the left hand and lighter in the right, until the last page is turned and the weight is distributed wholly to the left side for the first time, before it is put back on the table or returned to the shelf. This subtle shift of balance has been going on ever since that barely discernible equatorial distinction between the page before the middle of the book and the page after. From then on in everything is downhill, so to speak, with the gradient of that hill palpably present throughout the later pages of a reading that is timed and I would suggest, emotionally tuned, to this shift. Tuned because we are preparing ourselves for a leave-taking from characters we thought we knew, characters we have attended to, accompanied in and out of the dark nights of the novel. Taking leave of April and Frank Wheeler as played by Kate Winslet and Leonardo di Caprio in the film of the novel by Sam Mendes has quite a different dynamic when we are asked to put our gaze upon their departure from the illuminated limits of a screen, with which we have no tactile relation save the immersion in an acoustic envelope engineered by Thomas Dolby. That has no spine, no dorsal regard, unlike this.

I am not here evoking a sense of an ending, a closing time to end up at that terminus called "late work", following Edward Said's late reflections on late work before he became "the late Edward Said". All that boils down to in the end is a form of "Tempest Studies" in which theatres planning a makeover announce their season will end with that last great play and hope that the Shakespearian symmetry will pay off with the offer of more hands, more applause. There are no biographical interests for me here in this first instance of ending (either personal or architectural), rather what it feels like to "sense an ending" and then to experience that ending, aesthetically, in the constructed realm of things that are made and upon which we are asked to put our gaze.

I am especially interested in this specific closing context in the peculiar ethical dilemma such a sense of an ending brings about in the theatre, that is where customers pay to sit in seats in the dark while something happens on some boards in front of them raised slightly from the ground under some form of artificial lighting. This peculiar arrangement has been referred to as the "bourgeois stage" and my proposition here is that as a machine of representation it "does" good ending. Its rhythms, its formal properties are preparations *for* such endings which distinguishes it from contemporary practices of duration and continuity, sampling, infinite rearrangement, a shuffle culture in which keeping going is celebrated at all costs over closure. The show must go on. . . . My simple suggestion here, and it is almost too trite to reveal so summarily, is that the sense of an ending one experiences in the theatre is an ethical encounter with all other endings one has known and will know. It is a rehearsal for, and a reiteration of, such endings and in this curious propensity to face forward towards light while receiving the past through one's back to the dark, turns around Paul Klee's storm tossed angelic figure, invites Walter Benjamin's "angel of history" to peer into a past that as a stage is the back end of the future that awaits us outside, on the road.

Last Orders

In 2006 the Chicago-based performance ensemble Goat Island's director Lin Hixson announced, in a form of epistle to the company and then their audiences, the nature of their ending. After 22 years of collective practice this recognition and generous embrace of a "last order" allows us to cast back from a future date of ending to ask: "what becomes us in closure?" This announcement by Goat Island was suspended in an apparently elegant openness unable to hide its brutal, *irreparable*, underside epithet, "we quit", the ultimate performative for a performance company. This was of course not the first aesthetic auto-destructive act to tease the presumptuous logic of aesthetic repair. It joins an eminent lineage of self-imposed artistic breakdowns. The artist Gustave Metzger was some time ago an apogee of such dissimulations – he tended to blow himself up in galleries. In 1968 Keith Arnatt, in a two-second piece spread nightly over ten weeks of German television called *Self Burial*, gradually and with a remarkable lack of ceremony buried himself in a hole in the ground. But given the commitment by Goat Island to a fiercely material and ecological understanding of *repair* and its significance, to acknowledge an *end*, an irreparable condition by definition, exposes their last collective work, *The Lastmaker*, to a different kind of attention.

The announcement by Lin Hixson, on 4 June 2006, characteristically linked finality and formality: "We want to provide an example of ending, of lastness . . . We have thus derived a directive for our new piece concerning lastness, which we place alongside the other concerns of the piece."[3] Unlike William Forsythe, who had just two years before "closed" his *corps Ballet Frankfurt* on the withdrawal of significant funding from the local Frankfurt authorities, there were from Goat Island *no appeals* to save them from their better judgement, nor to register on some web site our outrage at the calamity of their closure.

This *dis-closure* arose from a legacy of work that had, with unusual sensitivity, concerned itself most rigorously with a spare choreography of rehabilitation, rescue and recovery, of an overtly politicized and yet never political aesthetic treatment of a dominant, hegemonic super power in an age of retreat and right-wing retrenchment. There was a sense in which the announcement of this ending of an aesthetic and pedagogic adventure of the most exhilarating kind was materially bound to the manner of other closures to come and how we might think them and activate or *distance* them. The implication that an essentially *aesthetic* announcement of ending has wider implications than its immediate impact within a relatively enclosed community of audiences, will take some explaining. It has something to do with being human, the ethical animal who is ethical because it has to ask "how to act", and not some other kind of creature who *knows* how to act (Read, 2008; Ridout, 2009).

Late Human

When Brian Saner, a long-moving member of the company, worked as he always did between the floor, unlikely elevation and the caring manipulation of objects (almost always wooden objects) he accompanied these choreographic passages with apparently winsome stories and sometimes popular songs. I liked the way that all the members of the company moved together in the spaces I saw their work, in a gymnasium in Reading, in a warehouse in Chicago, in a school assembly hall in Nottingham, at Battersea Arts Centre and the Chelsea Theatre in London, but I am drawn to Brian's movement, now in my head, or whatever part of us choreographic memory inhabits, perhaps for the model it offers of an intimate act of repair and recovery conveyed upon an object that then is enticed into performing itself for us. There is nothing didactic in this show whatsoever, but the far-fetched sense of a *proxy performance* seems closer in this theatre company than any other I have witnessed. I think this is something to do with the precise manner in which the company questioned among themselves, over relatively extended periods of project development, the legitimacy of prevailing claims to our attention and then skewed these preoccupations towards apparently naturalized objects, issues and ideas that in movements neither seismic nor semiotic but rather *seamless* were stitched back into the fabric of our senses of the world.

It is this seamless effect, stitched from materials that by all accounts should not be patched together, that allowed a Goat Island event to oscillate between the two imaginary poles of the natural and historical so *effortfully*. There *is* labour and it is palpable – it is unlikely that a tall, well-built man could defy gravity otherwise – but the entry of Brian Saner to a collective of dancing is effected not by expanding the terms on which that most rigid of categories once relied, but rather exposing those terms themselves to some careful thought to establish how they already accommodate a diversity of practices. To imagine that this choreographic "distribution of the sensible" is any less fiercely policed than any other would be naïve. But the "stitch" that I once saw Brian Saner suffer in a breathless moment of recovery, following but clearly at "the end of" a particularly energetic klaxon-accompanied work-out in *Sea & Poison* might be the acidic clue to how the *nature* of these seams have been exposed through history. It took the sequence to finish after an unlikely sequence of recapitulations and reprises for its formal achievements to come into view, to be felt.

The Franciscan Model

I would like to compare that seamless exposure of effort with another kind of end, a "rend" in something that continues to try to achieve its own end but is continuously interrupted from this purpose by the generosity of curators wishing to extend its life for "just one more show".[4] *The Lastmaker*, Goat Island's cobbled-together swansong, was, perhaps predictably, the show that made everyone who saw it wish Goat Island would "go on". It was particularly appreciated for Mark Jeffery's evocation of St Francis of Assisi in the form of a pathetic imitation of Larry Grayson – pathetic in the true sense: moving, stirring, suffering, as well as the obvious newer sense of feeble. While we were clearly meant to be suffering his confused presence, his suffering in that car crash of identity crisis was palpable. It dogged his timing, it would not be catty to say it was the pits, it was bull. But, like the best kind of school production that *despite itself* glows with representational excess and illuminated truths, this mincing ur-saint provided a rend in the image machine, it provided a way to look inside the workings at why ending something might just be for the best. Put it out of its misery, go on, put it down, now!

But in so doing, in all this putting down I was wishing on it as it stuttered to its planky conclusion, it "took me back", or perhaps I should say it simply for the first time made me *aware of my back*, suspended, not quite wholly connected to my front in a dark hallway that some years before had been a place of my comings and goings, a beginning of sorts. It rendered something that was not without struggle, for the performer no less than me within this "box of representation". This is how Georges Didi-Huberman explains this process:

> The frontality where the image placed before us suddenly rends, but the rend in its turn becomes frontality; a frontality that holds us in suspense, motionless, we who, for an instant, no longer know what to see under the gaze of this image. Then we are before the image as before the unintelligible exuberance of a visual event. (2009: 228)

The crisis that was unravelling before me in the form of the exuberance of a performer whose grasp on one verbal reality was tenuous to say the least, never mind the unholy trinity we were being offered here (a 13th-century holy peripatetic, a 20th-century second rate comic, a dancer who spoke weakly more than moved sweetly) secured my gaze on a rend within which there were two striking images that somehow entered through my back without me needing to turn around to look at the road from which they had come. They entered accompanied by a figure who while bearing no likeness to the confused trinity I saw before me somehow had already completed their performances for them.

This was the history that came to mind "backed up", you might say, from that sense of an ending. My grandfather spent his retirement from the Civil Service in acts of mowing, neighbourhood charity and prayer. In this he was at least part-human, for as Cioran (1998: 169) said: "Man certainly began praying long before he knew how to speak, for the pangs he must have suffered upon leaving animality, upon denying it, could not have been endured without grunts and groans, prefigurations, premonitory signs of prayer." He had two religious icons in his hallway, one a large, dark, portrait of St Christopher carrying a small child with a halo across a torrential river. The lustrous depths of the painting were unfathomable from below, but helpfully my grandfather had cut three characters from the newspaper, "M", "r" and ".", and stuck them with glue over the "St." on the brass title plate. The excommunication, or demotion of Christofero by the Vatican, from saint to secular, had galvanized in my grandfather some seriously contrary hagiography of this child-bearing commoner.

Beneath the painting on a small hall table stood a foot-high plaster statue of St Francis. In his customary brown habit, hooded and encircled with white birds, with creatures at his sandaled feet, this half religious, half secular hybrid stood as a reminder to the possibility of being marginal without being heretic, revolutionary without being nihilistic, spiritual and ecological (Le Goff, 2004). The Franciscans were more concerned with what "lay beyond" than the holiness, or not, of the towns, especially caring for the well-being of those new immigrants from that beyond, a lay society that Jacques Le Goff (2004: 5) describes as becoming increasingly active in religious life between 1250 and 1300 in Umbria. These lay movements read the Bible in the vernacular and actively distinguished between *aperta*, those narratives accessible to all, and *profunda*, those dogmatic statements reserved for the clergy.

My grandfather liked him for all this, but especially because he didn't like the privacy of confession. From the 12th century, the *collective* act of lay confession common to St Francis, and the assembled distribution of penance, became for the first time a private act of whispering into the ear of a priest. I suspect this incarcerated, over-occupied chamber reminded my grandfather too much of other ghosts in the machine for which he was responsible, other public secrets that he would have just preferred to have been public knowledge. Francis was not a miracle-maker, rather the liver of an exemplary life. Indeed the showy virtue of miracle enactments was for the first time, through Francis, subordinated to an everyday engagement with suffering and loss, repair and reaffirmation. Instead of these miracles, Francis was marked by a certain performance prosaicness, he "stood out from his companions as a minstrel, a jongleur" (Le Goff, 2004: 24). He was the first Christian to carry the stigmata but was so embarrassed by them that he began to travel by donkey covering himself in his characteristically modest robes. He was also unusual for the number of women he knew and his choice to keep their constant company.

St Francis was there, in the happy hallway of my grandfather's home, because of his affirmation of joy against the morose *accedia* in sadness of his monkish forbears, self-obsessing and dedicated to their tears. He was of course, quickly followed by the reassertion of masochistic Christianity that characterized the Catholicism I left for theatre. I was attracted to this statue and what it appeared to stand for during a strange time at school when my writing became too small to read. Francis too rejected bibliographies and books whose materialism was risking the secular, chivalrous culture of the oral troubadours (Le Goff, 2004: 61). Books by contrast were luxury items for possession rather than distribution. And of course, above all, his was a pedestrian movement, breaking with the isolation of monasticism, for whom the poor meant the poor. Francis loved the family not in some contemporary, banal binary tension with the individual, but in its more radical unsettling of the "Order". And in an age that paid no attention to children, minors were central to his wandering world; he was, for my grandfather at least, the coming community.

Francis' hands were crossed, not in prayer, but as though pulled in opposite directions by the animals around them, like a straitjacket across his habit. He was humanized by being less than he once was, a plaster cast-off, the loss of some fingers to the birds, so the direction of this ambidextrous coming and going was difficult to ascertain. His destination would appear to have been neither nature nor culture, there was no destination in that hallway, but the threshold of a human venue where premature endings could always begin again for those who arrived too late, the posthumous ones who were always in the process of beginning again.

Early Animal

For the figure who has to ask how to act, a peculiar symmetry between an ethical and theatrical dilemma that afflicts the human animal is complicated here by a figure for whom acting is only identified as more or less affinity *with* animality. Franciscanism is the forbear of the early-Modern revolution in the rendition of that animality and without that movement the Renaissance might never have found a representative means to figure animals as anything but less than human. Without that movement, artists would have continued to be as unfaithful to the portrayal of the animal as they had been since the cave.

Take, for instance just one example of such a historical seam, offered by the eighth-century Iraqi literary scholar al-Jahiz, in his monumental work *The Book of Living Things*. This encyclopaedic work of the medieval Arabo-Islamic world provides us with a surprisingly modern account of what Daniel Heller-Roazen (2005) has called the "lesser animal". The lesser animal is of course, following the logic of the recent widespread interest in the innovative capacity of performance to fail and fail better, the human. For the human let us for the moment recall Mark Jeffery's St Francis, as played by Larry Grayson, setting down some sweet but stupid wind-up birds at the periphery of the playing space of *The Lastmaker.*

Al-Jahiz was a great admirer of animals; that was not unusual, for their abilities and wonders were commonly written about in the 800s. But, unlike Aristotle, it is the precision of the comparison with human animals that makes most interesting reading here. Animals are flawless while man is, by implication, *deeply flawed*. But irrespective of the discipline and education that human animals endure, al-Jahiz is in no doubt as to their inability to accomplish spontaneously that which animals achieve naturally. In turn, for al-Jahiz the human therefore "remains the lesser animal among living beings" (Heller-Roazen, 2005: 131).

Doing less in this instance is an invitation to think in what ways this might mean, well, less. Animals are unable, because perfect, to do failure. For al-Jahiz, and I quote: "Man is made in such a way that when he accomplishes an act that is difficult to carry out, he has the ability to do one that is less difficult" (quoted in Heller-Roazen, 2005: 131). This is a power of performance, al-Jahiz says, that God has granted to man and man alone. There is no such possibility nor "performance capability" for animals; the performance of the *easier act* is beyond them. This is why they were trusted to work in circuses, and this is why the funny act with the little dog that bypasses the flaming hoop and runs round the side, while its pack exerts themselves flying through the air, is so haunting. This lesser act has required by definition more, not less, training against the animal's exemplary instincts.

Birds could not be Beatles because while melodic, harmonious and rhythmic they are not able to sing a *lesser song*. It is only because they were able to put *Yellow Submarine* on the same album as other divinely inspirational tracks such as *Eleanor Rigby* that the Beatles marked themselves out as aesthetic creatures. The "distribution of the sensible", as Jacques Ranciere framed it, that determines who is in a position to engage with aesthetic acts through seeing, listening or speaking, cannot even get going without this simple, rather minor, fact being acknowledged.

> Al-Jahiz suggested that the essence of human action lies in this possibility of *reduction*; however small or great, a human act owes its consistency to its capacity to be less than itself. It follows that one cannot understand any work of man on its own. To grasp a human action as such, one must look to the shadows of the more minor acts it inevitably projects around it: to those unaccomplished acts that are less than it and that could always have been performed in its stead, or, alternately, to those unaccomplished acts with respect to which it itself is less than it could have been. (Heller-Roazen, 2005: 132)

I think this has been put more eloquently by Gilles Deleuze in his exploration of a minor literature and indeed by Matthew Goulish in his recent work on the ordinary and the idea of meiosis, that is *lessening* for dramatic effect.

But what does this have to do with Mark Jeffery and *The Lastmaker*? I would propose that theatre is the venue where the recollection of the lesser animal, *as the lesser animal*, makes conscious and subjectivizes its participants as *actively limited*. This is the rend in the image fabric that is torn and then sutured by our invitation to look in and repair. Franz Kafka, the epitome of a minoritarian author, offers us an aphorism that illuminates the relationship between such recollection and lesser acts in a startling way in a short story. His protagonist says:

> I can swim just like the others. Only I have a better memory than the others. I have *not forgotten* the former *inability to swim*. But since I have not forgotten it, being able to swim is of no help to me; and so, after all, I cannot swim. (quoted in Heller-Roazen, 2005: 146)

Though lesser, as a non-swimmer, by the end of this paradox, Kafka's unidentified narrator is better for it, conscious of a lesser time when unable to swim subtracts from her current status as a swimmer among others. The infernal memory of Goat Island passages that simultaneously undo themselves as they build themselves is not far from this "unswum swimmer".

The End

But what happens when those albeit lesser things *end*, when the open, the coming community, the expanded collective becomes closed? Theatres "go dark" but what if they were to "stay dark"? If theatre has a vocabulary it is surely an insanely *hopeful* one: "opening night", "corpsing" (turning a death into a synonym for uncontrollable laughter) and "resting" as in out of work and depressingly under-employed are indicative of the eternal optimism of the theatre mind. Philosophically the language adopted by theatre theory is no less affirmative. Natalist terms, pregnant with expectation, are delivered by philosophical midwives: "birth to presence", "emergent appearance", "becoming". I suppose it was all this *untrammelled joy* that in the end got the nascent discipline of performance studies down so seriously in the 1990s and prompted its thanatalogical excesses.

But what, without submitting ourselves to the ever present performance studies couch, about the potential *finality* of this exchange, *extinction itself* as the ultimate un-dialectical event for the author and the actor? Such propositions as Goat Island and their contemporaries have shown us, are not all dead ends. In *Theatre and Everyday Life* (Read, 1993) I undertook a survey of what I called the "first human venue", *the everyday*, and demonstrated how theatre had become removed from the everyday in return for its privileges as a cultural artefact. It had traded its origins for a specious respectability among other excised arts practices with which it had little affinity. The status of theatre often rested on the maintenance of these distances rather than their recognition. In the second part of that book I wrote about the relations between the *given* and the *created*, pointing out that beneath the depths of the everyday lay an even more threatening remainder to cultural production, *the natural*, which if admitted might overwhelm all the coordinates of what performance might be considered to be. When I said *inundation*, I *did* mean drowning, but not quite in the spirit that the philosopher Adi Ophir means when he says: "The planet of the drowning is our planet" (Ophir, 2005: 625).

The Last Human Venue

I was fearful of that inundation myself and I did not take this further at the time. Later, in *Theatre, Intimacy and Engagement* (Read, 2008), I took up that task and did so in the company of the *theatre* examples of Goat Island, Forced Entertainment and Societas Raffaello Sanzio. The significance of what I call "the last human venue" in that book – that is, theatre in the age of urban modernity – is that this theatre, *our theatre*, has been the *first theatre* to understand itself as an "epochal theatre", with a sense of the *present*, yes, but also for the first time a sense of its newness is braided with a vivid sense of its *ending*. The whole point of this venue has been the way in which its *time* did not correspond with "its *times*" (see Ophir, 2005: 615). The relativist excuses of postmodern fragmentation cannot account for the simple fact that, as Adi Ophir put it, "In the present time, the end of the world appears as a common horizon of the whole world that determines a common future for this era" (2005: 619).

The whole *oeuvre* of Goat Island, but especially since their work more than a decade ago on *The Sea and Poison*, would appear to trace this common horizon through their working methods. The simultaneous production in London of *The End of Reality* by Richard Maxwell and *The World in Pictures* by Forced Entertainment in the Fall of 2006, announced through quite different aesthetics, yet strangely comparable atmospheres, a not disconnected sense of epochal finality. This sense of an ending could not *only* have been because my own interminable writing of a book was nearing a conclusion (though such confusions about the apparent symmetry between ones own rhythms of work and others should never be wholly excluded). Consider Jerry Killick's final soliloquy at the close of Forced Entertainment's troubling production of *The World In Pictures* in which he imagines for the audience their own disappearance in one hundred years, the disappearance of any memory of them in two hundred years, the disappearance of the theatre in a thousand years and the disappearance of the city in ten thousand years, and consider that this soliloquy is codaed by a hopeful epitaph. Smiling wryly he reminds us that the last two hours in our company has been a pleasure and wishes us a good-night.[5]

Such an end, as Martin Heidegger cautioned in his own writing on ending, would not be signified as an "event" but rather as a certain acceptance of *finitude*, an anticipation of it, as Goat Island and Jerry Killick have done, and not a *completion* of it (see Ophir, 2005: 620). It is this finitude that Adi Ophir describes as "laying a common ground". The difference between these endings and those of other eras is the degree to which they are no longer *eschatological* beliefs (eschatology as the *theological* discourses expressed as the present realization of last things). Rather it is predicated on the wholly secular, commonly available proliferating data of pollution and global-warming, represented through the present discourses of scientific truths. There is no messianic quality to the evening news but a rather prosaic adaptation to circumstance for the neo-human now wedded to a catalytic converter here, a low carbon-emission freezer there. Inconvenience has now become the key register of a certain future discomfort.

In The Event of Extinction

Extinction is available in, at least, three relatively accessible and well-documented contemporary modes: by nuclear accident or endeavour, by ecological disrepair and by the ratcheting up of mass exterminations common to genocides of the last century. Each has their own time and, apparently, site of conduct. But as Adi Ophir makes clear, however they operate, they would appear to converge at "an end". It is perhaps a petty solace to speculate whether it is *performance* or *thinking* that is extinguished first, just before this end, but such thoughts on theatrical closure certainly sharpens the tired debate regarding the relationship between practice and theory. If, as Ophir says, "The end is a being without witness" (2005: 624), then it is that witless, witness-less, condition that marks the end as one from which performance will be a relatively early casualty. In this sense it is quite the opposite of the saturated space of the witnessing of the end of all performances that I began with.

The late loss of witnesses reminds us that all of these modes of extinction *are* measurable, and are being actively measured, in the present era. There *are* attempts to measure nuclear proliferation, ecological disaster and the historical repetition of genocides as so many varieties of act and accident. And it is, perhaps inevitable that the arts, from Thom Yorke to Barney and Bjork are coralled in this end to play the siren warning to these apocalyptic scenarios. In the quite proscriptive words of Adi Ophir, "If there are still poetry, science and thinking, they should *sound to us* as the music played on board the Titanic *would have sounded* had the passengers only known *how* to see the iceberg" (2005: 625). The last human venue is the place where the position of the human animal in relation to such an end became measurable. We can, in Adi Ophir's affirmative prose, always estimate this distance through thinking and lengthen this distance, from or to an end, not only through acting, but through action, and here the distinction between the gerund and the verb is moot. It is not so much a question of how to act that is the ethical touchstone now, rather what forms of action, what shapes our conduct might take in acting on behalf of others for whom the suffering of images is no longer an aesthetic nicety.

The time that remains, in this scenario, would therefore appear to be one of *hope*. Having begun to measure these distances, having begun to act in the interests of their lengthening, the last human venue would appear to be a venue with a purpose, even if that purpose, in my imagination, always falls short of claims for the political. If the word venue in its original French form meant "a coming", then this place would appear to be the assembly of those before *any second coming*, any messianic or metaphysical aspiration to transcend the materiality of the threat of an ending. In the very face of this ethical *impotential*, as the human face is washed from the sand by the tides of day and night, the insistence of the potential that has to be inherent to any ending, is realized: the opportunity to return to the shore and draw out another human face is staged upon the sacrifice of a million sandy species that, for the Surrealist author Roger Caillois have long ago died in a "first and fatal intimacy".

Exit

The box glows green with the word I was looking for. It reminds us where we are if not who we are. It can never be turned off when we are there and we have no idea who turns it off when we are not. If ever they do. Sigmund Freud describes the composition of his last work *Moses and Monotheism* in recalcitrantly conventional theatrical terms. Close to death, on the publication of this concluding volume that "completes" his complete works in 1939, Freud noted in his diary: "Quite a worthy exit . . ." (Freud, 1992: 255). I wonder what makes an exit "worth" something and another less, or even nothing? I suspect it was what went before. But, unlike the summative remorselessly cumulative narrative of the talking cure, there is always an opportunity to recover oneself in the theatre, to begin again. Who after all in an aisle on the way towards that sign has not done an involuntary dance, a feint to block an interloper, a last look back to check the satisfying distance climbed, away from the stage towards the light of the "front of house" before the dark outside. Not the same "outside" but certainly the same stars that preside over those who, like animals leaving the ark, flee the Laurel Players' *The Petrified Forest*, on their way out towards their revolutionary road, the one that until the end of their world, and then the world, goes around and around:

> There was nothing to watch now but the massed faces of the audience as they pressed up the aisles and out the main doors. Anxious, round-eyes, two by two, they looked and moved as if a calm and orderly escape from this place had become the one great necessity of their lives; as if, in fact, they wouldn't be able to begin to live at all until they were out beyond the rumbling pink billows of exhaust and the crunching gravel of this parking lot, out where the black sky went up and up forever and there were hundreds of thousands of stars. (Yates, 1962: 10)

Notes

1 I have returned to some "loose ends" that were first developed in Read (1993) and Read (2008). I am grateful to their respective publishers for permission to return to this work and explore it in this new context, if of course, not to resolve it, and am grateful to the editor of this volume John Matthews for his invitation and insight.

2 The "illuminated stage" is a misheard appropriation of an idea developed by Joe Kelleher via Edmund Husserl and Søren Kierkegaard figured as "the illuminated theatre" and developed at "Traces of . . ." seminar series, King's College London, March 2010.

3 'Goat Island: A New Performance (Work in Progress)' company programme note for *Sacred* Season, Chelsea Theatre, London, September 2006.

4 See Didi-Hubermann (2005: 139–228) for a subtle exposition of the "rend" in art history.

5 The last night of the London run of *The World in Pictures*, Forced Entertainment, Riverside Studios, London, Saturday 18 November 2006.

References

Cioran, E. M. 1998. *The Trouble With Being Born.* Trans. Richard Howard. New York. Arcade.

Didi-Huberman, G. 2005. *Confronting Images.* Trans. John Goodman. University Park, PA. Pennsylvania State University Press.

Freud, Sigmund. 1992. *The Diary of Sigmund Freud 1929–1939: A Record of the Final Decade.* London. Hogarth Press.

Heller-Roazen, Daniel. 2005. *Echolalias: On the Forgetting of Language.* New York. Zone.

Le Goff, Jacques. 2004. *Saint Francis of Assisi.* Trans. Christine Rhone. London. Routledge.

Ophir, Adi. 2005. *The Order of Evils: Toward and Ontology of Morals.* New York. Zone.

Read, A. 1993. *Theatre and Everyday Life: An Ethics of Performance.* London. Routledge.
Read, A. 2008. *Theatre, Intimacy and Engagement: The Last Human Venue.* Basingstoke. Palgrave Macmillan.
Ridout, Nicholas. 2009. *Theatre and Ethics.* Basingstoke. Palgrave Macmillan.
Yates, Richard. 1962. *Revolutionary Road.* London. Deutsch.

CONTRIBUTORS

Simon Bayly is an artist and writer working broadly in the field of performance. He is a Principal Lecturer in Drama, Theatre and Performance at Roehampton University, where he teaches on the MA in Performance and Creative Research. Since 1992, he has directed the London-based live arts company PUR.

Anna Furse is a director, writer and performance researcher. Reader in Theatre and Performance at Goldsmiths, University of London, she directs the MA in Performance Making. She was Artistic Director of Paines Plough in the 1990s, and with her company Athletes of the Heart she currently works on international, interdisciplinary collaborations.

Adam Hosein is an Assistant Professor of Philosophy at the University of Colorado, Boulder. He has a BA from Merton College, Oxford and a PhD from MIT. He has been a fellow at Stanford University and the University of Chicago Law School.

Adrian Kear is a professor and Head of the Department of Theatre, Film and Television Studies at Aberystwyth University. His books include *Theatre and Event* (Palgrave Macmillan, forthcoming 2011), *Psychoanalysis and Performance* (with Patrick Campbell, Routledge 2001) and *Mourning Diana: Nation, Culture and the Performance of Grief* (with Deborah Lyn Steinberg, Routledge 1999). He is a contributing editor to *Performance Research* and writes regularly for the philosophical journal *Parallax.*

John Matthews is a Lecturer in Theatre and Performance at Plymouth University. He is a performer and theatre-maker and formerly Research Fellow of the Stanislavski Centre, he taught at Rose Bruford College of Theatre and Performance. John publishes research on training in sites including the rehearsal room, the clinic and the cloister and he is the author of *Training for Performance* (Methuen Drama, 2011) and *Anatomy of Performance Training* (Methuen Drama, 2014).

Alan Read is currently Professor of Theatre at King's College London where he directs the work of the Performance Foundation. He is the author of *Theatre & Everyday Life: An Ethics of Performance* (Routledge, 1993) and *Theatre, Intimacy & Engagement: The Last Human Venue* (Palgrave Macmillan, 2008).

Nicholas Ridout teaches in the Department of Drama at Queen Mary University of London. He is the author of *Stage Fright, Animals and Other Theatrical Problems* (Cambridge University Press, 2006) and of *Theatre & Ethics* (Palgrave Macmillan, 2009). He is the co-author, with Claudia Castellucci, Romeo Castellucci, Chiara Guidi and Joe Kelleher, of *The Theatre of Socìetas Raffaello Sanzio* (Routledge, 2007) and co-editor, with Joe Kelleher, of *Contemporary Theatres in Europe* (Routledge, 2006).

David Torevell is Associate Professor in Theology and Religious Studies at Liverpool Hope University. He is the author of *Losing the Sacred: Ritual, Modernity and Liturgical Reform* (T&T Clark, 2000), *Liturgy and the Beauty of the Unknown: Another Place* (Ashgate, 2007) and joint editor with Clive Palmer of *The Turn to Aesthetics: An Interdisciplinary Exchange in Applied and Philosophical Aesthetics* (Liverpool Hope University Press, 2008). Among his research interests are contemplative theology and spirituality. He is presently completing a study of the performative dimension of contemplative theology in dialogue with a new interpretation of Samuel Beckett's masterpiece *Waiting for Godot.*

INDEX